NATURE, MAN, AND WOMAN

ALAN W. WATTS

NATURE, MAN, AND WOMAN

46778

VINTAGE BOOKS

A Division of Random House

New York

To the beloved company of the stars, the moon, and the sun;
to ocean, air, and the silence of space;
to jungle, glacier, and desert,
soft earth, clear water, and fire on my hearth.
To a certain waterfall in a high forest;
to night rain upon the roof and the wide leaves,
grass in the wind, tumult of sparrows in a bush,
and eyes which give light to the day.

Contents

Preface

AS I LOOK AROUND MY LIBRARY I AM OFTEN
strangely troubled by the way in which my books fit so
snugly into categories. Most of my books have to do with
philosophy, psychology, and religion, and they represent
points of view from every great culture of the world.
Yet with an absolutely oppressive monotony they fit themselves into the stale dualities of philosophical and theological argument, varied from time to time with sensible and
uninspiring compromises. Volume after volume is so easily
identified as supernaturalist or naturalist, vitalist or mech-
anist, metaphysical or positivist, spiritualist or materialist,
and the compromise volumes are usually so watered down
as to be compilations of platitudes and sentimentalities.

Underlying all these dualities there seems to be a basic
division of opinion about those two great poles of human
thought, spirit and nature. Some people stand plainly "for"
one and "against" the other. Some stand mainly for one but
give the other a subordinate role. Others attempt to bring
the two together, though human thinking moves in such
firm ruts that it usually turns out that they have settled
inadvertently for one or the other. It is doubtless foolhardy
for any philosopher to claim that he has broken loose from
these ruts and at the same time said anything meaningful.
Discussion is so much a matter of juggling with categories
that to start breaking up the categories is usually to break
up the discussion.

But this is not just a matter of categories, logic, and phil-

osophical argument. The opposition of spirit and nature
is also a matter of life and feeling. Ever since I began to
study these matters I have been puzzled by the way in
which exponents of the life of the spirit do not seem to be
at home in nature and in their bodies, for even when they
do not identify the natural with the evil they damn it with
faint praise. So often I have sympathized with bold pagan
rebellion against this bodiless spirituality, and yet never
joined it because the final word of this "gather ye rosebuds
while ye may" philosophy is always despair—or some
fatuous utopianism which, because it is only a matter of
time, comes to the same thing. For the congenitally sick,
the victims of accident, the impoverished, and the dying
this philosophy has no message.

But is the alternative to joy in the body delight in the
discarnate spirit? I have been realizing more and more
that partisans to opposed philosophies share the same
premises, which are usually unconscious. Furthermore,
these premises are transmitted by such social institutions
as the structure of language and the learning of roles, in-
fluencing us in ways of which we are hardly aware. Thus
the conventional saint and the conventional sinner, the
ascetic and the sensualist, the metaphysician and the materialist may have so much in common that their opposition is quite trivial. Like alternating heat and cold, they
may be symptoms of the same fever.

Unconscious premises of this kind come to light when
we try to understand cultures very far removed from our
own. They too have their hidden assumptions, but when
we compare these cultures with our own the basic differences must at last become obvious. This is peculiarly true
of the cultures of the Far East, because they are high civ-
ilizations which arose in isolation from the West, developing patterns of thought and language startlingly different

from those of the Indo-European strain. Thus the value of
the study of Chinese language and thought is not simply
that we ought to be able to communicate with the Chinese
people, important as this is. It is rather that Chinese studies tell us so much about ourselves, for the very reason
that of all the advanced cultures of the world this is the
most unlike our own in its ways of thinking.

Thus it was always such a delight to me that Chinese
philosophy would never quite fit into the ruts of Western,
and even Indian, thought, and this was pre-eminently true
of the problem of spirit and nature. For there were no categories of Chinese thought corresponding to spirit and nature as we understand them. Here was a culture in which
the conflict between spirit and nature hardly existed, a
culture where the most "naturalistic" painting and poetry
were precisely the most "spiritual" of its art forms.

This book is not, however, a formal account of the
Chinese philosophy of nature. I have discussed this at
length in my previous book, *The Way of Zen*, and it has
been marvellously illuminated by Joseph Needham in his
Science and Civilization in China. My object here is not
to expound and compare philosophical systems; it is to reflect upon a great human problem in the light of the Chinese view of nature, especially as it was expressed by Lao-
tzu and Chuang-tzu. The urgency of the problem of man's
relation to nature and the general intent of this book are,
I think, sufficiently discussed in the Introduction which
follows. Here I have also explained why the problem of
man's relation to nature raises the problem of man's relation to woman—a matter about which the spiritually-
minded members of our own culture have been signifi-
cantly squeamish.

Because this book is one in which I am frankly "thinking
out loud," I would like to repeat some remarks from the

Preface to my *Supreme Identity*. "I am not one who believes that it is any necessary virtue in the philosopher
to spend his life defending a consistent position. It is
surely a kind of spiritual pride to refrain from 'thinking out
loud,' and to be unwilling to let a thesis appear in print
until you are prepared to champion it to the death. Philosophy, like science, is a social function, for a man cannot
think rightly alone, and the philosopher must publish his
thought as much to learn from criticism as to contribute
to the sum of wisdom. If, then, I sometimes make state-
ments in an authoritative and dogmatic manner, it is for
the sake of clarity rather than from the desire to pose as
an oracle."

There is the prevalent belief in the West that intellectual and philosophical pursuits are unessential ornaments of culture of far less value than active and technological accomplishments. This attitude is in great danger
of being confused with the Eastern view that real knowledge is nonverbal and beyond the reach of concepts. But
our actions are almost invariably directed by a philosophy
of ends and values, and to the extent that this is unconscious it is liable to be bad philosophy with disastrous
active consequences. The so-called "nonintellectuality" of
the East lies as far above thought as mere activism lies
below it. Such knowledge cannot be reached by making
one's concepts unconscious under the impression that one
is sacrificing the intellect. Distorting premises can be abandoned only by those who go down to the roots of their
thinking and find out what they are.

ALAN W. WATTS

Mill Valley, California
February, 1958

Introduction

A FLOOR OF MANY-COLORED PEBBLES LIES
beneath clear water, with fish at first noticed only by
their shadows, hanging motionless or flashing through the
liquid, ever-changing net of sunlight. We can watch it for
hours, taken clear out of time and our own urgent history,
by a scene which has been going on just like this for
perhaps two million years. At times, it catches us right
below the heart with an ache of nostalgia and delight com-
pounded, when it seems that this is, after all, the world
of sane, enduring reality from which we are somehow in
exile.

But the feeling does not last because we *know* better.
We know that the fish swim in constant fear of their lives,
that they hang motionless so as not to be seen, and dart into
motion because they are just nerves, startled into a jump
by the tiniest ghost of an alarm. We know that the "love
of nature" is a sentimental fascination with surfaces—that
the gulls do not float in the sky for delight but in watchful
hunger for fish, that the golden bees do not dream in the
lilies but call as routinely for honey as collection agents
for rent, and that the squirrels romping, as it seems, freely
and joyously through the branches, are just frustrated little
balls of appetite and fear. We know that the peaceful
rationality, the relaxed culture, and the easy normality of
civilized human life are a crust of habit repressing emotions too violent or poignant for most of us to stand—the
first resting place which life has found in its arduous climb

1

from the primordial, natural world of relentless struggle and terror.

But we *think* we know, for this robustly realistic, tough-guy picture is as much a re-creation of the natural world in our own image as the most romantic and escapist of country ecstasies. Our view of nature is largely a matter of changing intellectual and literary fashions, for it has become a world strangely alien to us. This estrangement is intensified in a time and a culture wherein it is widely believed that we must depart from the principles which have hitherto governed the evolution of life. For it is felt that the future organization of the world can no longer be left to the complex and subtle processes of natural balance from which life and man himself arose. When the process brought forth human intelligence, it introduced an entirely new principle of order. From now on, it is claimed, the organization of life cannot *happen;* it must be *controlled,* however intricate the task. In this task the human intellect will no longer be able to rely upon the innate and natural "wisdom" of the organism which produced it. It will have to stand alone, relying strictly upon its own resources. Whether he likes it or not, man—or rather the conscious intelligence of man—must henceforth rule the world.

This is an astonishing jump to conclusions for a being who knows so little about himself, and who will even admit that such sciences of the intelligence as psychology and neurology are not beyond the stage of preliminary dabbling. For if we do not know even how we manage to be conscious and intelligent, it is most rash to assume that we know what the role of conscious intelligence will be, and still more that it is competent to order the world.

It is this very ignorance of and, indeed, estrangement from ourselves which explains our feeling of isolation from nature. We are, as it were, cut asunder into a confined center of attentiveness, which is "I," and a vast organic complexity which we know only in terms of indescribable and disquieting feelings, or abstract biological technicalities: and this is "myself." Throughout his history, the type of man molded by the Western cultures has been peculiarly estranged from himself, and thus from the natural environment in which his organism inheres. Christian philosophy, which knows so much about the nature of God, has so little to say about the nature of man, for beside its precise and voluminous definitions of the Holy Trinity stand the vaguest and briefest descriptions of the human soul and spirit. The body, grudgingly admitted to be good because it is God's handiwork, has in practice been viewed as territory captured by the Devil, and the study of human nature has been mostly the study of its foibles. In this respect the psychologists have faithfully followed the theologians.

For the scientist, despite his theoretical naturalism, tends to regard nature, human and otherwise, as a world to be conquered and reordered, to be made subject to the technology of the rational intellect, which has somehow disowned and shaken off its roots in the very organism it now presumes to improve. In practice, the technical, rational consciousness is as alien to the natural man as was the supernatural soul. For both alike, nature and the natural man is an object, studied always by a technique which makes it external and therefore different from the subjective observer. For when no knowledge is held to be respectable which is not objective knowledge, what we know will always seem to be *not* ourselves, not the subject. Thus we have the feeling of knowing things only from the outside, never from within, of being confronted eternally with a world of impenetrable surfaces within surfaces within surfaces. No wonder, then, that our ideas of

what nature is like on the inside are guesses at the mercy
of fashion.

In some ways, however, the temper of scientific thought
is far less managing and imperious than it was at the beginning of this century, if only because greater knowledge
brings with it an awareness of ignorance. At the same
time, even from the most coldly intellectual point of
view, it becomes clearer and clearer that we do not live
in a divided world. The harsh divisions of spirit and
nature, mind and body, subject and object, controller and
controlled are seen more and more to be awkward conventions of language. These are misleading and clumsy
terms for describing a world in which all events seem to
be mutually interdependent—an immense complexity of
subtly balanced relationships which, like an endless knot,
has no loose end from which it can be untangled and put
in supposed order.

It is not that spirit has been reduced to nature, or to
what "nature" used to mean, or that the mind has been
reduced to the body. We have less and less use for words
which denote stuffs, entities, and substances, for mind and
matter have together disappeared into *process*. Things
have become events, and we think of them in terms of pattern, configuration, or structure, no longer finding any
meaning in the question, "Of what stuff is this pattern
made?" But the important point is that a world of interdependent relationships, where things are intelligible only
in terms of each other, is a seamless unity. In such a world
it is impossible to consider man apart from nature, as an
exiled spirit which controls this world by having its roots
in another. Man is himself a loop in the endless knot, and
as he pulls in one direction he finds that he is pulled from
another and cannot find the origin of the impulse. For
the mold of his thoughts prevents him. He has an idea of

himself, the subject, and of nature, the object. If he cannot find the source of the impulse in either, he is confused. He cannot settle for voluntarism and he cannot settle for determinism. But the confusion lies in the tangle of his thoughts rather than the convolutions of the knot.

Yet in the present atmosphere of Western thought the realization of man's total involvement with nature is perhaps depressing. It is humiliating for a culture which always used to think of man as nature's head and lord. Even now, despite ever louder voices of warning, the culture still revels in technical power. Contrary to its avowed philosophy of living for the future, its perspective is really no longer than the day after tomorrow, for it exploits the resources of the earth and the energies of radioactivity with only the most fragmentary knowledge of the complex relationships so disturbed. The apparently depressing thing is not merely that the universe is not to be pushed heedlessly around, but that the very state of mind in which we attempt to do so is an illusion. For if man is one with nature in a seamless unity, his beneficent ideals must after all be rationalizations of the great primordial forces of lust and terror, of blind striving for survival, which we believe to be the basic impulses of nature.

But before we decide to be depressed we could learn to know nature from the inside. The discovery of our total involvement is momentous, so that the understanding of the character and inner working of the endless knot is the most important of all philosophical inquiries. As already suggested, we might find out that our notions of blind primordial urges are pure mythology. Might it not be that they are fashions in anthropomorphic thinking which have simply swung to the opposite pole from the older notion that the primordial impulse was the will of a personal and beneficent God? The very ideas of impulses, forces, motivations, and urges may be nothing more than abstract intellectual ghosts as impalpable as the mysterious "it" in the sentence, "It is raining." The same grammatic convention which requires subjects for verbs may be the sole reason for urges and drives behind actions. Yet such a line of thought may be even more disturbing, since it suggests a universe of life which has no motive at all—not even survival—and surely an absolutely purposeless world would be the most depressing of all possibilities.

But the idea of a purposeless world is horrifying because it is incomplete. Purpose is a pre-eminently human attribute. To say that the world has no purpose is to say that it is not human, or, as the *Tao Tê Ching* puts it:

> *Heaven and earth are not human-hearted* [jen].

But it continues:

> *The sage is not human-hearted.* v

For what is not human appears to be inhuman only when man sets himself over against nature, for then the inhumanity of nature seems to deny man, and its purposelessness to deny his purposes. But to say that nature is not human and has no purpose is not to say what it has instead. The human body as a whole is not a hand, but it does not for this reason deny the hand.

It is obviously the purest anthropomorphism to assume that the absence of a human quality in bird, cloud, or star is the presence of a total blank, or to assume that what is not conscious is merely unconscious. Nature is not necessarily arranged in accordance with the system of mutually exclusive alternatives which characterize our language and logic. Furthermore, may it not be that when we speak of nature as blind, and of matter-energy as unintelligent, we are simply projecting upon them the blankness which we feel when we try to know our own consciousness as an object, when we try to see our own eyes or taste our own tongues?

There is much to suggest that when human beings acquired the powers of conscious attention and rational thought they became so fascinated with these new tools that they forgot all else, like chickens hypnotized with their beaks to a chalk line. Our total sensitivity became identified with these partial functions so that we lost the ability to feel nature from the inside, and, more, to feel the seamless unity of ourselves and the world. Our philosophy of action falls into the alternatives of voluntarism and determinism, freedom and fate, because we have no sense of the wholeness of the endless knot and of the identity of its actions and ours. As Freud said:

> Originally the ego includes everything, later it detaches from itself the external world. The ego-feeling we are aware of now is thus only a shrunken vestige of a far more extensive feeling—a feeling which embraced the universe and expressed an inseparable connection of the ego with the external world.[1]

If this be true, we must not think of the hungers and fears of the plants and beasts in terms of our own exclusively egocentric style of awareness, for which the fate of the separated ego is the all-consuming interest because it is felt to be all that we are. Our difficulty is not that we have developed conscious attention but that we have lost the wider style of feeling which should be its background, the feeling which would let us know what nature is from the inside. Perhaps some intimation of this lost feeling underlies our perennial nostalgia for the "natural life," and the myth of a golden age from which we have fallen.

[1] Freud (1), p. 13.

There may be no reason to believe that a return to the lost feeling will cost us the sacrifice of the individualized consciousness, for the two are not incompatible. We can see an individual leaf in all its clarity without losing sight of its relation to the tree. The difference between ourselves and the animals is possibly that they have only the most rudimentary form of the individualized consciousness but a high degree of sensitivity to the endless knot of nature. If so, the extreme insecurity of their lives is by no means as intolerable as it would be for us.[2] Without some such compensation, it is hard to see how forms of life other than man could have found the game of life worth the candle for so many millions of years.

In coming to an understanding of nature in which man is to be something more than a frustrated outsider one of our most valuable sources of insight is the Taoist tradition of Chinese philosophy, with its outgrowths in Zen Buddhism and Neo-Confucianism. In the second volume of his *Science and Civilization in China* Joseph Needham has indicated many points at which the Chinese philosophy of nature is of the utmost relevance to the inquiries of modern science and philosophy, and some of these need to be explored. The standpoint of Taoism is of special interest and value because it is a form of naturalism entirely different from our own mechanistic and vitalistic naturalisms, avoiding their antimetaphysical bias and their simplist reductions of nature to systems of abstraction which have absolutely nothing in common with what the Chinese mean by nature.

[2] Do the rapid and "nervous" motions with which animals avoid danger indicate that they are actually afraid? Human city-dwellers are just as agile in dodging traffic and negotiating superhighways, yet carry on all the darting and twisting required with relative unconcern. And what about the numberless neural adjustments whose lightning action keeps us from falling when we walk or run, from choking when we eat, and from being concussed when we play ball games?

Furthermore, the Taoist philosophy of nature is much more than a theoretical system—indeed, it is hardly this at all. It is primarily a way of life in which the original sense of the seamless unity of nature is restored without the loss of individual consciousness. It involves a new style of human action in relation to the environment, a new attitude to technical skills whereby man seems to interfere artificially with the natural world. It requires a fundamental revision of the very roots of our common sense, especially with respect to such matters as the instinct for survival, the pursuit of the good and the pleasurable to the elimination of the evil and painful, and of the function of effort and discipline, or will power, in creative action.

For our purposes, however, the best way of exploring the Chinese philosophy of nature is not to embark upon a systematic and historical account of Taoism.[2] It is better to introduce it as one goes along in a general discussion of the relation of man to nature which will also clarify the Western attitude to the problem.

Of central importance in any such discussion are the actual means whereby awareness of the seamless unity may be discovered, since this whole inquiry is in the realm of feeling rather than thought, and is in the spirit of poetry rather than formal, intellective philosophy. But the so-called means of discovery are apparently problematic and paradoxical since the lost awareness is found by "no means." Actions of the will or ego can only strengthen its divided mode of consciousness, and at first sight this is extremely frustrating for one who knows no other way of action. Yet we are familiar enough with the insincerity and contradiction of trying to be natural, the more so when it is most urgent that we should act naturally and without

[2] Which would in any case be a rather un-Taoistic procedure, although it has been admirably done by Holmes Welch in his recent *Parting of the Way*, for which see Welch (1).

self-consciousness. The Taoist idea of naturalness goes far beyond the merely normal, or the simply unostentatious way of behaving. It is the concrete realization that all our experiences and actions are movements of the Tao, the way of nature, the endless knot, including the very experience of being an individual, a knowing subject.

The Chinese phrase which is ordinarily translated as "nature" is *tzu-jan*, literally "of itself so," and thus a better equivalent might be "spontaneity." This is almost Aristotle's idea of God as the unmoved mover, for nature in both whole and part is not regarded as being moved by any external agency. Every movement in the endless knot is a movement of the knot, acting as a total organism, though the parts, or loops, of the knot are not looked upon as passive entities moved by the whole. For they are parts only figuratively divided from the whole for purposes of recognition and discussion; in reality, the loops are the knot, differences within identity like the two sides of a coin, neither of which can be removed without removing the other.[4] Thus all art and artifice, all human action, is felt to be the same as natural or spontaneous action—a world-feeling marvellously expressed in Chinese poetry and landscape painting, whose technique involves the fascinating discipline of the "controlled accident," of doing exactly the right thing without force or self-conscious intention.

The techniques of Far Eastern art are, however, somewhat exotic to serve as illustrations for Western people of the application of this philosophy of nature. Yet the specific application of the philosophy should be discussed, and, for a number of reasons, it has seemed that the most

[4] An even better illustration might be the Möbius strip, a paper tape formed into a ring with a single twist. It clearly has two faces, and yet they are identical.

suitable subject for this discussion is the relationship of man and woman, especially in its sexual phase. For one thing, there is an obvious symbolic correlation between man's attitude to nature and man's attitude to woman. However fanciful this symbolism may sometimes be, it has in fact had an enormous influence upon sexual love in both Eastern and Western cultures. For another, sexual love is a troubled and problematic relationship in cultures where there is a strong sense of man's separation from nature, especially when the realm of nature is felt to be inferior or contaminated with evil. Needless to say, the Christian, and particularly the Anglo-Saxon, cultures are preoccupied with sexuality in ways that strike outsiders as peculiarly odd, and we ourselves are well aware that we have "sex on the brain" to an extraordinary degree. We are not going to solve this preoccupation by trying to forget about it, which has been the advice of our moralists for two thousand years. Nor will it yield to treatment at a narrowly medical or psychiatric level, as if it were a purely biological affair.

Above all, sexual love is the most intense and dramatic of the common ways in which a human being comes into union and conscious relationship with something outside himself. It is, furthermore, the most vivid of man's customary expressions of his organic spontaneity, the most positive and creative occasion of his being transported by something beyond his conscious will. We need hardly wonder, then, that cultures in which the individual feels isolated from nature are also cultures wherein men feel squeamish about the sexual relationship, often regarding it as degrading and evil—especially for those dedicated to the life of the spirit.

The disordered sexuality of the Western (and some other) cultures is surely due to the fact that the sexual relationship has never been seriously integrated with and illumined by a philosophy of life. It has had no effective contact with the realm of spiritual experience. It has never even achieved the dignity of an art, as in the Indian *Kamasutra*, and would thus seem to rank in our estimation far below cookery. Theoretically, the Christian sacrament of Holy Matrimony is supposed to sanctify the relationship, but in practice it does so only by indirection and by prohibitions. We have dubbed the relationship "animal," and animal we have for the most part let it remain. Matrimony has not so much ennobled it as fenced it in, trusting naïvely that "true love" would somehow find a way to make the relationship whole and holy. And this might indeed have come to pass, without introducing any studied techniques, given the presence of certain other conditions. It might have come to pass of itself, spontaneously, if the culture had known anything of real spontaneity. But this was, and is, impossible when human personality is centered exclusively in the ego, which in its turn is set over against nature as the dissociated soul or mind. Generally speaking, the style of philosophy which we have followed and the type of spiritual experience which we have cultivated have not lent themselves to a constructive application to sexuality.

It is good for a man not to touch a woman. . . . I say therefore to the unmarried and widows, "It is good for them if they abide even as I." But if they cannot contain, let them marry; for it is better to marry than to burn. . . . But and if thou marry, thou hast not sinned; and if a virgin marry, she hath not sinned. Nevertheless such shall have trouble in the flesh [or, perhaps better, with the flesh]. . . . But this I say, brethren, the time is short: it remaineth, that both they that have wives be as though they had none. . . . I would have you without preoccupation. He that is unmarried careth for the things that belong to the Lord, how he may please the Lord. But he that is married careth for the things that are of the world, how he may please his wife.[5]

This grudging toleration of sexuality as an unbearable pressure which, sometimes and under strict conditions, has to be released puts it on the level of an urge to stool, of a regrettable vestige of animality, happily to be left behind in the Kingdom of Heaven. As such it has no positive relation whatsoever to the life of the spirit.

But fortunately for the growth of Christian spirituality, St. Paul gave these words as advice and not as a commandment. For they are offset, in the sacred scriptures, with the Song of Songs, which has thus far been interpreted allegorically in terms of "the spiritual marriage betwixt Christ and his Church," or between Christ and the soul. As we shall see, there are potentialities in the Christian heritage not only for the development of sexual love in matrimony as a means to the contemplative life, but also for resolving the basic rift between spirit and nature which has so troubled the Christian cultures of the West.

The approved academic method of studying the sexual implications of the Taoist philosophy of nature would, presumably, be to investigate the erotic customs and literature of the Far East. But in place of such a difficult and time-consuming task there is a simple and practical short cut: to understand the basic principles of the philosophy and apply them directly to the problem. Other than this, there is no clear way of approach, for in the Far East the influence of Taoist philosophy upon the mass culture has always been in 'irect. Actual followers of the philosophy, as distinct from the organized Tao'st religion, which is a very different affair, have been relatively few. Documents do

[5] St. Paul in 1 Corinthians, 7.

indeed exist about Taoist sexual practices, but they savor more of the psychophysiological theories of the Taoist religion than of the nature philosophy of Lao-tzu and Chuang-tzu. Even so, the general tenor of these documents is approximately what one would imagine the sexual application of the Taoist philosophy to be. Furthermore, even at the mass level, sexual love in the Far Eastern cultures appears to be far less problematic than with us, for there is no doubt that the Taoist feeling of the naturalness of the human state has, however indirectly, had a wide influence upon the everyday life of the people.

Other Asian traditions than the Taoist have much to contribute to both aspects of our inquiry. Various trends of Hindu philosophy, which seem, however, to be submerged in modern times, illuminate the theme with a marvellous symbology which has been interpreted with such deep insight in the works of Heinrich Zimmer. As to the crucial problem of realizing or feeling the seamless unity of nature, nowhere is there anything more direct, simple, and concrete than the approach of Zen Buddhism—the way of life which has contributed so much to the profound nature philosophy of the Japanese.

It is tragic that at a time when these universally human insights nurtured in Asia "speak to our condition" so appropriately, the Asian peoples themselves are associated in our minds with rampant nationalisms which we are feeling as a serious political threat. Unhappily, it is probably far more serious than we have yet recognized. But is it of any use to point out that they have learned these political philosophies, by reaction, from us, and that, in their differing ways, Gandhi, Nehru, Nasser, Mao Tse-tung, and the other leaders of Asian nationalism are to a large degree Western in both personality and doctrine? Almost every one of them is a product of an educational system established by Western colonialism, and their political philosophies and ambitions are remote indeed from the principles of statecraft set forward in the *Tao Tê Ching*.

Less and less has the "wisdom of the East" anything to do with modern Asia, with the geographical and political boundaries of the world which such terms as East and West, Asia, Europe, and America, now represent. More and more "the East" as a source of wisdom stands for something not geographical but inward, for a perennial philosophy which, in varying forms, has been the possession of traditional, nonhistorical cultures in all parts of the world. For the spiritual contrast of East and West is really a contrast between two styles of culture, two radically different categories of social institutions, which never really corresponded to the contrast of Europe and Asia as geographical divisions.

We might call these two types of culture progressive and historical on the one hand, and traditional and nonhistorical on the other. For the philosophy of the first is that human society is on the move, that the political state is a biological organism whose destiny is to grow and expand. Examining the record of its past, the progressive society reconstructs it as history, that is, as a significant series of events which constitute a destiny, a motion toward specific temporal goals for the society as a whole. The fabricators of such histories easily forget that their selection of "significant" events from the record is subjectively determined—largely by the need to justify the immediate political steps which they have in mind. History exists as a force because it is created or invented here and now.

On the other hand, traditional societies are nonhistorical in that they do not imagine themselves to be in linear motion toward temporal goals. Their records are not histories but simple chronicles which delineate no pattern in human events other than a kind of cycling like the rotation of the seasons. Their political philosophy is to maintain the balance of nature upon which the human community depends, and which is expressed in public rites celebrating the timeless correspondences between the social order and the order of the universe.

Thus the focus of interest in the traditional society is not the future but the present, "the still point of the turning world." All their artifacts are made for the immediate material advantage of the thing itself, rather than for abstract monetary profit, or for such purely psychological byproducts as prestige or success. Such artifacts are therefore made unhurriedly through and through; they are not fine surfaces slapped together, with every imaginable short cut on the inside. On the other hand, the progressive workman has his eye on the clock—on the play which is to come when the work is over, on the leisure society which is to follow the completion of the Five-Year Plan. He therefore rushes to complete artifacts which, for that very reason, are not worth playing with when playtime comes. Like a spoiled child, he soon tires of his toys (which is exactly what most of his products are),[6] and is wooed back to work by the prospect of ever more sensational (as distinct from material) gimmicks to, come.

For it is strictly incorrect to think of the progressive cultures as materialistic, if the materialist is one who loves concrete materials. No modern city looks as if it were made by people who love material. The truth is rather that progressive man hates material and does everything possible to obliterate its resistances, its spatial and temporal limits. Increasingly his world consists of end-points, of destinations and goals with the times and spaces between them

---

[6] The Cadillac or Thunderbird automobile of this date being essentially a toy rocket-ship rather than a convenient means of transportation.

eliminated by jet propulsion. Consequently there is little material satisfaction in reaching the goal, since a life full of goals or end-points is like trying to abate one's hunger by eating merely the two precise ends of a banana. The concrete reality of the banana is, on the contrary, all that lies between the two ends, the journey as it were, all that jet propulsion cuts out. Furthermore, when the time and space between destinations are cut out, all destinations tend to become ever more similar. The more rapidly we can travel to Hawaii or Japan or Sicily, the more rapidly the resort is, as tourists say, "spoiled," which means that it is increasingly like Los Angeles, Chicago, or London.

Once again, we see that the goals of progressive men are actually psychological and spiritual, the sensations, kicks, and boosts for which material realities are merely the unfortunately necessary occasions. His hatred of materiality is the continuing expression of the basic rift between his ego and nature. In the sexual sphere the goal is not so much the concrete personality of the woman as the orgasm which she provokes, and provokes not so much as an integral woman as an aggregation of stylized lips, busts, and buttocks—woman in the abstract rather than this or that particular woman. As de Rougemont has pointed out so clearly in his *Love in the Western World*,[7] such love is not the love of woman but the love of being in love, expressing a dualistic, dissociated, spirit-loving and matter-hating attitude to life. But no less short-circuited and antinatural is the conception of love which makes future procreation its sole end, especially because what, in this conception, is to be procreated is another *soul*,

---

[7] De Rougemont (1). At a later point it will be necessary to take issue with some of the historical aspects of this remarkable work, which has managed to foist upon historical Christianity a doctrine of love which is really a modern and novel development of Christianity that would probably have horrified the Patristic age.

willy-nilly attached to a body which it will never be really permissible to enjoy. Here, too, we see the essential continuity of the Western attitude from historical Christianity to modern "paganism."

Underlying this continuity is the fact that, as one might say, both God and the Devil subscribe to the same philosophy since both inhabit a cosmology where spirit stands against nature. Furthermore, the architects of this cosmology were unaware of the mutual interdependence, or correlativity, of opposites, which is the principal reason why they did not perceive the inner identity of spirit and nature, subject and object, and why they did not notice the hidden compact between God and the Devil to reproduce one another. They did not notice it even when, as the conceptions of the two became fully elaborated, they sometimes exchanged characters so that the image of God became diabolical and the image of the Devil divine. For as the image of God was composed of goodness piled on goodness, power piled on power, it became insufferable and monstrous. But in conceiving the image of the Devil there were no laws to be kept, and the creative imagination could run riot, emptying all its repressed and sensuous contents. Hence the persistent allure of Satanism and the fascination of evil.

When the mutual interdependence of the opposites is not seen, it becomes possible to dream of a state of affairs in which life exists without death, good without evil, pleasure without pain, and light without darkness. The subject, the soul, can be set free from the concrete limitations of the object, the body. Thus in the Christian doctrine of the resurrection of the body, the body is usually considered to be so transformed by the spirit that it is no longer in any real sense a body. It is rather a fantasy-body from which all the really earthy qualities have been taken away—weightless, sexless, and ageless. The idea that the good can be wrested from the evil, that life can be delivered permanently from death, is the seed-thought of the progressive and historical cultures. Since their appearance, history seems to have taken a sudden leap forward, and, in a few centuries, the conditions of human life have been under radical and ever faster change, though hitherto they had remained relatively constant for millennia.

However, it is not so much that history has taken a sudden leap forward as that, with the progressive cultures, history has come into being. The partisans of historical culture seem to congratulate themselves on having escaped from cyclic into linear time, from a static into a dynamic and "on-going" world order—failing to see that nothing is so cyclic as a vicious circle. A world where one can go more and more easily and rapidly to places that are less and less worth visiting, and produce an ever-growing volume of ever-less-nourishing food, is, to cite only the mildest examples, a vicious circle. The essence of a vicious circle is that one is pursuing, or running away from, a terminus which is inseparable from its opposite, and that so long as this is unrecognized the chase gets faster and faster. The sudden outburst of history in the last five hundred years might strike one as more of a cancer than an orderly growth.

The foregoing might well seem the prelude to a doctrine of revolution. But it is nothing of the kind. Nothing is further from our intent than to advocate a return to the traditional style of culture and an abandonment of the progressive. The fallacy of all traditionalist or "back-to-nature" romanticisms is that they are themselves progressive, looking to a future state of affairs which is better than the present. Just as the ego can do nothing to overcome its own isolated mode of consciousness, the community can do nothing *in order* to deliver itself from the progressive fallacy, for this would be the contradiction of affected naturalness. The "goal" of a traditional culture is not the future but the present. That is to say, it lays its material and practical plans for food and shelter in the days and years to come, but no more. It does not aim at the psychological enjoyment which the future meals will bring. In a word, it does not pursue happiness.

Furthermore, the wiser members of such cultures do not even seek enjoyment from the present moment. For in the instant that one grasps the moment to get something from it, it seems to disappear. The reason is perhaps that enjoyment is a function of nerves rather than muscles, and that nerves receive automatically and passively, whereas muscles grasp actively. Enjoyment is always gratuitous and can come no other way than of itself, spontaneously. To try to force it is, furthermore, to try to experience the future before it has arrived, to seek the psychological *result* of attending to the present experience and thus short-circuiting or cutting out the experience itself. Obviously, however, the person who attempts to get something from his present experience feels divided from it. He is the subject and it is the object. He does not see that he *is* that experience, and that trying to get something from it is merely self-pursuit.

Ordinarily we think of self-consciousness as the subject's awareness of itself. We would be far less confused if we saw that it is the subject-object's awareness of itself. For the knower is what he knows in somewhat the same way as the seemingly two surfaces of the Möbius strip are one. Pushing the analogy a little further, conscious experiencing seems to be a field which, like the strip, twists back upon itself:

It is not, then, that I know both other things and myself. It is rather that the total field I-know-this knows itself.

While this problem of our awareness of the present will receive fuller attention at a later point, it is necessary at least to see the principle of it here so that we may understand the illusion of making an attempt to get something from life in the sense of a good, happy, or pleasant psychological state. For the point is not, in our accustomed egocentric mode of thinking, that it would be good to return to our original integrity with nature. The point is that it is simply impossible to get away from it, however vividly we may imagine that we have done so. Similarly, it is impossible to experience the future and not to experience the present. But trying to realize this is another attempt to experience the future. Some logician may object that this is a merely tautological statement which has no consequence, and he will be right. But we are not looking for a consequence. We are no longer saying "So what?" to everything, as if the only importance of our present experience were in what it is leading to, as if we should constantly interrupt a dancer, saying, "Now just where are you going, and what, exactly, is the meaning of all these movements?"

There is, indeed, a place for commentary, for interpretations of nature and predictions of its future course. But we need to know what we are talking about, which requires a primary background of contemplation and inward silence, of watching without questions and jumping to conclusions. May we go back, then, to the floor of pebbles beneath the water and the fish in the sunlight's rippling net . . . and watch?

I: MAN AND NATURE

1: Urbanism and Paganism

WHEN CHRISTIANS FIRST DISTINGUISHED
themselves from pagans, the word "pagan" meant "country-dweller." For the first centers of Christianity in the
Roman Empire were the great cities—Antioch, Corinth,
Ephesus, Alexandria, and Rome itself. Furthermore, during the centuries in which Christianity was born and
spread throughout the Empire, the growing mercantile
wealth of Rome was attracting population to the cities, so
that as early as 37 B.C. the government of the Emperor
Augustus showed concern for the decline of agriculture.
The *Georgics* of Vergil were a direct expression of this
concern—poems written at the behest of the government
in praise of the rural life:

> *O fortunatos nimium, sua si bona norint*
> *Agricolas!*

Blest, aye, blest to excess, knew they how goodly the portion
Earth giveth her farmers!

That Christianity grew up in the cities, at a time when,
as today, the big city was the center of economic and
cultural attraction, is a circumstance which must have had
a deep influence upon the whole character of the religion.
For Christianity as a whole has a decidedly urban style,
and this is true not only of Roman Catholicism but also of
Protestantism, which first arose in the burgher cities of
Western Europe. In evangelizing the West, the main dif-

ficulty which Christianity encountered was, for as long as fifteen hundred years, the competition of the tenacious nature religions of the peasantry.

Perhaps it is easiest to express the effect of these circumstances upon Christianity in the form of a personal impression, not, I believe, at all peculiar to myself. For as long as I can remember, I have been puzzled by the fact that I can feel like a Christian only when I am indoors. As soon as I get into the open air, I feel entirely out of relation with everything that goes on in a church—including both the worship and the theology. It is not as if I disliked being in church. On the contrary, I spent much of my boyhood in the precincts of one of Europe's most noble cathedrals, and I have never recovered from its spell. Romanesque and Gothic architecture, Gregorian chant, medieval glass and illuminated manuscripts, the smell of frankincense or of the mere must of ancient stone, and, above all, the ritual of the Mass—these are as magical for me as for the most ardent Catholic romanticist. Nor am I insensible to the profundities and splendors of Christian philosophy and theology, and I am well aware that early training implanted in me the bitter-sweetness of a Christian conscience. But all this is in a watertight compartment, or rather, in a closed sanctuary where the light of the open sky comes only through the symbolic jewelry of stained-glass windows.

It is often said that the aesthetic atmosphere of Christianity is a mere irrelevance. The Christian life is not what one feels, but what one wills, usually in the teeth of one's feelings. The contemplative mystic would say that to know God is precisely not to feel him; it is to know him by the love of the will in a "cloud of unknowing," in the dark night of the spirit where, to sense and feeling, God is utterly absent. Therefore he who knows Christianity in terms largely of its aesthetic glamour knows it not at all.

> Illuminated missals—spires—
> Wide screens and decorated quires—
> All these I loved, and on my knees
> I thanked myself for knowing these
> And watched the morning sunlight pass
> Through richly stained Victorian glass
> And in the colour-shafted air
> I, kneeling, thought the Lord was there.
> Now, lying in the gathering mist,
> I know that Lord did not exist.[1]

Yet this denial of feeling, while heroic, manly, and robust, is yet another symptom of what I am trying to express— of the fact that the Christian world, as we know it, is only a half-world in which the feeling and the symbolically feminine is unassimilated. Feeling, as a means of judgment and knowledge, is misleading to those who do not know how to use it, through lack of exercise and cultivation. Furthermore, in a milieu where feeling is underestimated or disregarded, its expressions are all the more revealing of the underlying state of mind.

It has, then, been my impression that there is a deep and quite extraordinary incompatibility between the atmosphere of Christianity and the atmosphere of the natural world. It has seemed well-nigh impossible to relate God the Father, Jesus Christ, the angels, and the saints to the universe in which I actually live. Looking at trees and rocks, at the sky with its clouds or stars, at the sea, or at a naked human body, I find myself in a world where this

[1] John Betjeman, "Before the Anaesthetic or A Real Fright," in *Selected Poems*. John Murray, London, 1948.

religion simply does not fit. Indeed, it is a characteristically
Christian attitude to confirm this impression, since "my
kingdom is not of this world." Yet if God made this world,
how is it possible to feel so powerful a difference of style
between the God of church and altar, for all his splendor,
and the world of the open sky? No one would dream of
attributing a landscape by Sesshu to Constable, or a sym-
phony by Hindemith to Haydn. In the same way, I have
found it a basic impossibility to associate the author of the
Christian religion with the author of the physical universe.
This is not a judgment as to the relative merits of the two
styles; it is only to say that they are not by the same hand,
and that they do not mix well together.

This has, of course, been felt before, and there is an
argument to explain it. It is said that whereas the beauty
and the style of the physical world is natural, the beauty
of Christianity is supernatural. The nearest thing in the
physical world to supernatural beauty is the beauty of the
human being, and more especially of the human mind.
Christianity suggests the urban rather than rural atmosphere because in the former we are surrounded by works
of the mind. While it is true that all creatures under the
sky are the works of God, man, and even the works of
man, are far higher works of God than anything else. They
reveal more of the character of God than the sun, moon,
and stars, for what we sometimes call the artificial is
nearer to the supernatural than to the natural.

It is easy, this argument would continue, to love the
aesthetic surfaces of nature, so long as we do not have to
contend with the ruthless heartlessness, the cold struggle
for life, which underlies it. But it is in man alone that
there have arisen ethical and moral ideas which, as it were,
give nature a feeling heart—and this, again, goes to show
that God is reflected in nature nowhere so clearly as in

man. It is true that we sometimes need to seek relief from
the hideousness of crowds and cities in the solitudes of
nature, but this is only because the worst is the corruption
of the best. The evil of man far exceeds the evil of the
spider or the shark, but only because the goodness of man
immeasurably exceeds the goodness of a spring landscape.
One has only to consider how cold and desolate the fairest
face of nature can seem to a man left utterly alone, willing
to exchange the whole sum of natural beauty for a single
human face.

Making a still stronger point, the argument could go on
to say that however poor the fit between Christianity and
nature, nowhere is there a religion so perfectly in accord
with human nature. By and large, the naturalistic religions
hold out for man no greater hope than a philosophic acceptance of the inevitable, a noble but sorrowful resigna-
tion to the truth that nature is beyond good and evil, and
that death is the necessary counterpart of life, as pain of
pleasure. But this sacrifices the most human thing about
man—his eternal, childlike hope that somehow, someday,
the deepest yearnings of his heart will come true. Who is
so proud and unfeeling that he will not admit that he
would not be deliriously happy if, by some strange magic,
these deep and ingrained longings could be fulfilled? If
there were everlasting life beyond death after all? If there
were eternal reunion with the people we have loved? If,
forever and ever, there were the vision and the union of
hearts with a God whose beatitude exceeds immeasurably
the most intense joy that we have known—somehow including all the variety of form and color, uniqueness and
individuality, that we value so much upon earth? Christianity alone, it would be argued, has the audacity to affirm
this basic hope which the wisdom of the world represses,
and so is the only fundamentally joyous religion. For it

gambles, recklessly, upon the scheme of things turning out to be the best that we hope for, challenging man to put the whole might of his faith in the idea that his nature, at its most human, is made in the image of the ultimate reality, God. . . . And, it might be added, if we lose the gamble, we shall never know that we have lost.

This is not, perhaps, the most profound version of the final ideal at which Christianity aims. It is, however, representative. For in discussing the attitude of Christianity to nature, I am not exploring as yet the deepest resources of the Christian tradition. I am trying to state the attitude of Christianity as it has been held by large numbers of intelligent people, and thus as it has been an influential force in Western culture. The individual Christian will sometimes protest in reading the following pages that this or that is not how he understands Christianity, and he may feel in particular that the presentation is theologically immature. But I have found that when Christian theologians become subtle and mystical, and sometimes when pressed in conversation to say what they *really* mean, it becomes increasingly difficult to tell the difference between Christianity and, say, Vedanta. Here, however, we are discussing the characteristics which make Christianity unique, and the majority of intelligent Christians who take their religion in a partisan way do indeed insist upon its uniqueness—even when their knowledge of other traditions is rudimentary. We are discussing, above all, the atmosphere, the quality of feeling, which Christianity involves, and which is so influential upon the culture. So powerful is the sway of this feeling quality that, in practice, the individual often yields to it even when his intellectual grasp of the faith is extremely mature. And the appeal of Christianity is to very human and very powerful feelings—the love of man for his own kind, the bedrock of nostalgia for home and one's own people, coupled with the fascination of the heroic, the challenge to believe in the possibility of an ultimate victory over evil and pain. In the face of this appeal, the non-Christian may be tempted to feel like a spoilsport or a skeleton at the banquet.

But the premise of the argument is just that, in his heart of hearts, man *does* feel alien from nature, and that his very deepest longing is for an eternity of joy, to the exclusion of sadness and suffering. As even Nietzsche said in *Zarathustra*:

> All joys want eternity,
> Want deep, profound eternity.

Yet to hold that these are ultimate and universal facts of human nature and feeling is to reveal a form of self-awareness which is still close to the surface, and a readiness to confuse what one feels as a result of social conditioning with what one feels absolutely and necessarily. The more a person knows of himself, the more he will hesitate to define his nature and to assert what he must necessarily feel, and the more he will be astounded at his capacity to feel in unsuspected and unpredictable ways. Still more will this be so if he learns to explore, or feel deeply into, his negative states of feeling—his loneliness, sorrow, grief, depression, or fear—without trying to escape from them.

In many so-called primitive cultures it is a requirement of tribal initiation to spend a lengthy period alone in the forests or mountains, a period of coming to terms with the solitude and nonhumanity of nature so as to discover who, or what, one really is—a discovery hardly possible while the community is telling you what you are, or ought to be. He may discover, for instance, that loneliness is the masked fear of an unknown which is himself, and that the alien-looking aspect of nature is a projection upon the forests of his fear of stepping outside habitual and conditioned patterns of feeling. There is much evidence to show that for anyone who passes through the barrier of loneliness, the sense of individual isolation bursts, almost by dint of its own intensity, into the "all-feeling" of identity with the universe. One may pooh-pooh this as "nature mysticism" or "pantheism," but it should be obvious that a feeling of this kind corresponds better with a universe of mutually interdependent processes and relations than with a universe of distinct, blocklike entities.

The more deeply we understand the play of our feelings, the more, too, we realize their ambivalence—the strange polarity of joy and sorrow, love and hate, humility and pride, elation and depression. We find that our feelings are not fixed, unrelated states, but slowly or rapidly swinging motions such that a perpetuity of joy would be as meaningless as the notion of swinging only to the right. In other words, just because it is static, a perpetual feeling is not a feeling, so that the conception of the perpetually good is a verbal abstraction which can neither be imagined, felt, nor actually desired. Such an idea can, once more, be taken seriously only by those who have not thoroughly explored the nature of feeling, who are unrelated to the natural realities of the very humanity which they hold to be God's image.

We begin, then, to discern the reasons why Christianity as we have known it differs so profoundly in style from the natural universe. To a large extent it is a construction of ideas or concepts playing together on their own, without adequate relation to that world of nature which ideas represent. It is true, of course, that in mathematics and physics we find purely conceptual constructions and ideas for which we can discover no sensuous image, such as curved space or quanta. But, in physics at least, these ideas are related to the physical world by testing their use in predicting the course of events. Furthermore, the physicist does not maintain that such ideas necessarily represent any concrete reality. He sees them rather as tools, like compasses, rulers, or numbers, which enable us to handle and measure that reality—tools which are not found but invented.

May it not be, then, that many of the central ideas of Christianity are creative inventions, like the cities in which they were nurtured? This would of course be true of any religion or philosophy to the extent that it is a system of ideas, especially of ideas that cannot be verified by an appeal to experience. But Christianity differs sharply at this point from other traditions, such as Buddhism and the Vedanta. In the latter, ideas play a very secondary part, for the real center of these traditions is an ineffable experience, which is to say an experience which is concrete and nonverbal, not an idea at all. In Christianity, however, the stress is upon belief rather than experience, and immense importance has always been attached to an acceptance of the correct formulation of a dogma, doctrine, or rite. Early in its history Christianity rejected *gnosis,* or direct experience of God, in favor of *pistis,* or the trust of the will in certain revealed propositions about God.

Spirit, then, is distinguished from nature as the abstract from the concrete, and the things of the spirit are identified with the things of the mind—with the world of words and thought-symbols—which are then seen, not as representing the concrete world, but as underlying it. For "in the beginning was the Word," God the Son conceived as the Divine Idea after whose pattern the universe was made. Thus the realm of concepts acquires not only an independent life of its own, but a life more real and more fundamental than that of nonverbal nature. Ideas do not represent nature, but nature represents ideas in the clogging vesture of material stuff. Hence what is impossible and unimaginable in nature is possible in idea—as that the positive may be separated permanently from polarity with the negative, and joy from interdependence with sorrow. In short, purely verbal possibility is considered as having a higher reality than physical possibility. It is hard not to feel that this is the power of thought running away with itself and getting out of hand, and defending itself against the charge of nonsense by asserting that its own reality is primordial, and nature but its clumsy copy.

Things are separable in words which are inseparable in nature because words are counters and classifiers which can be arranged in any order. The word "being" is formally separate from the word "nothing," as "pleasure" from "pain." But in nature being and nothing, or solid and space, constitute a relationship as inseparable as back and front. In the same way, the formally static character of our words for feelings conceals the fact (or better, the event) that our feelings are directions rather than states, and that in the realm of direction there is no North without South.

In the great Asian traditions, however, spirit—as Brahman or Tao—is less easily confused with the abstract. Spirit is found in the direct experience of the concrete, natural world in what Buddhists would call its "suchness" (*tathata*), that is, in its nonverbal and nonconceptual state. This is not, however, what we mean by the world in its material or physical state, for, as we shall see, the word "material" stands for the world as "metered" or measured —the nonverbal world represented in terms of distinct facts, things, and events, which, like feet and inches, are human inventions for handling and describing the world. There is no word for *what* the world is in its natural, nonverbal state. For the question "What is it?" is really asking, "In what class is it?" Now it should be obvious that classification is, again, a human invention, and that the natural world is not given to us in a classified form, in cans with labels. When we ask what anything is in its natural state, the only answer can be to point to it directly, suggesting that the questioner observe it with a silent mind.

Silent observation of this kind is exactly what is meant here by feeling (as distinct from particular feelings), the attitude and approach whereby nature must be explored if we are to recover our original sense of integrity with the natural world. In Taoism and Zen this attitude is called *kuan*, or "wordless contemplation." Just as one must sometimes be silent in order to hear what others have to say, so thought itself must be silent if it is to think about anything other than itself. We need hardly be surprised if, in default of this silence, our minds begin to be haunted by words about words about words. It is a short step from this to the fantasy that the word is prior to nature itself, when, in fact, it is only prior to the *classification* of nature—to the sorting of nature into things and events. For it is things, not the natural world itself, which are created by the word. But, for lack of mental silence, the two are confused.

The spell of words is by no means an enchantment to which only the intellectual is disposed. The most simple-minded people are as easily its prey, and it would seem that, at all levels of society, the cultures in which Christianity has arisen have been peculiarly confused by the powerful instrument of language. It has run away with them like a new gadget with a child, so that excessive verbal communication is really the characteristic disease of the West. We are simply unable to stop it, for when we are not talking to others we are compulsively thinking, that is, talking subvocally to ourselves. Communication has become a nervous habit, and cultures strike us as mysterious and baffling which do not at once tell all, or, worse, expect us to understand certain things without being told. I shall never forget the Japanese artist Hasegawa yelling in exasperation at the endless request for explanations from his Western students, "What's the matter with you! Can't you *feel?*"

For one type of culture, then, the "truth about nature" is the verbal explanation or reconstruction of the world, considered as a system of law which precedes and underlies it as the plan in the mind of the architect comes before the building of a house. But for another type it is nature itself, experienced directly in mental silence, which in Zen Buddhism is called *wu-nien* or "no-thought." [2] Thus in the cultures of the Far East we rarely find the discrepancy between religion and nature so characteristic of the West. On the contrary, the finest Buddhist and Taoist art of China and Japan is not, as one might suppose, concerned with formally religious themes, but landscape painting, and studies of birds, trees, rocks, and plants. Furthermore, Zen is applied directly to the technique of gardening, and to a style of architecture which deliberately integrates the house with its natural surroundings—which simultaneously encloses man and admits nature. These, rather than Buddha images, express the knowledge of ultimate reality.

And here we might mention a curious and apparently trivial symptom of the rift, not only between Christianity and nature, but also between Christianity and the natu-

---

[2] But this is not what we should call "thoughtlessness" or mere empty-mindedness. For thoughts are themselves in and of nature, and *kuan*, or wordless contemplation, can persist even in the midst of thinking. *Kuan* is therefore an absence of "mental mitosis," of the mind constantly trying to split itself, trying simultaneously to act and reflect, to think and to think about thinking, and so setting up the infinite regression or vicious circle of "words about words about words."

ralistic art forms of the Far East. Strangely enough, it is almost impossible to represent the central symbol of Christianity, the Cross or Crucifixion, in the Chinese style of painting. It has been tried many times, but never succeeds, for the symmetrical form of the Cross completely destroys the rhythm of a Chinese painting if it is made the principal image in the picture. Chinese Christians have tried to solve the problem by painting rustic Crosses with bark, twigs, and moss still on the wood. But those two straight beams simply jar with the rest of the painting, and, without destroying the symbol of the Cross, the artist cannot follow his natural tendency to bend the straight lines irregularly. For he follows nature in loving forms that are flowing, jagged, and unsymmetrical—forms eminently suited to his media, the soft brush and black ink. But in the art forms of Christianity, such as the Byzantine and Gothic, we find a love for the architectural and the courtly. God is conceived in the image of a throned monarch, and the rituals of the Church are patterned after the court ceremonials of the Greco-Roman emperors. Likewise, in the ancient Hebrew religion, the Ark of the Covenant was essentially a throne, hidden in the inner sanctuary of the Holy of Holies, which was built in the form of a perfect cube—symbol of completeness and perfection.

Yet from the standpoint of Chinese philosophy and aesthetics, this symmetrical and architectonic perfection is rigid and lifeless. Such forms are found but rarely in nature, and thus when the Chinese artist starts to paint the rigid Cross he finds himself in conflict, for what he really wants to paint is a living tree. Furthermore, he thinks of the power behind nature, not in the image of a monarch, but as the Tao—the way, course, or flow of nature—and finds images for it in water and wind, in the air and sky, as well as in the processes of growth. There was no sense that the Tao had any inclination to obtrude itself or to shine in glory like a monarch, but rather to work hidden and unknown, making it appear that all its achievements were the work of others. In the words of Lao-tzu:

> *The great Tao flows everywhere,*
> *to the left and to the right.*
> *All things depend upon it to exist,*
> *and it does not abandon them.*
> *To its accomplishments it lays no claim.*
> *It loves and nourishes all things,*
> *but does not lord it over them.* xxxiv

On the other hand:

His eyes were as a flame of fire, and on his head were many crowns; and he had a name written, that no man knew, but he himself. And he was clothed with a vesture dipped in blood: and his name is called the Word of God. . . . And out of his mouth goeth a sharp sword, that with it he should smite the nations: and he shall rule them with a rod of iron; and he treadeth the winepress of the fierceness and wrath of Almighty God. And he hath on his vesture and on his thigh a name written: KING OF KINGS, AND LORD OF LORDS.[3]

Magnificent as this is, the style is utterly different from the Taoist conception of the monarch, who is to

> *Blunt his sharpness;*
> *Get rid of his separateness;*
> *Soften his brilliance;*
> *Be even with the dust.*
> *This is called the profound identity.*[4] lvi

For,

> *The ruler who wants to be above the people must speak*
> *of himself as below them.*

---

[3] Revelation 19, 12–16.
[4] That is, the profound (or mysterious) identity of man and nature.

*If he wants to be ahead of the people, he must keep
    himself behind them.*
*Thus when the sage is above, the people do not feel
    him as a burden;*
*When he is ahead, the people do not feel him as a
    hindrance.* lxvi

The king takes his pattern from the Tao, not the Tao from
the king. And the Tao is always anonymous and unknown,
and the incessant changefulness and flowing imperma-
nence of nature is seen as a symbol of the fact that the Tao
can never be grasped or conceived in any fixed form.

The architectonic and artificial style of Christianity is
nowhere clearer than in the idea of God as the *maker* of
the world, and thus of the world itself as an artifact which
has been constructed in accordance with a plan, and which
has, therefore, a purpose and an explanation. But the mode
of action of the Tao is called *wu-wei*, translatable both as
"nonstriving" and "nonmaking." For from the standpoint of
Taoist philosophy natural forms are not made but *grown*,
and there is a radical difference between the organic and
the mechanical. Things which are made, such as houses,
furniture, and machines, are an assemblage of parts put
together, or shaped, like sculpture, from the outside in-
wards. But things which grow shape themselves from
within outwards. They are not assemblages of originally
distinct parts; they partition themselves, elaborating their
own structure from the whole to the parts, from the simple
to the complex.

It is fascinating to watch the formation of nature's most
unnatural-looking object—the crystal. For it does not appear in the solution piece by piece but altogether at once,
as if it were a projected image gradually coming into
focus upon a screen. Similarly, the lines of force in a mag-
netic field do not appear serially, as in drawing, but con-

stellate themselves in the iron filings as if a thousand hands were drawing them simultaneously—all in perfect co-ordination. Even when such an object as a plant-stem grows linearly, it does not do so by mere addition, as one builds a wall of bricks or pours concrete. The whole form expands from within, and this direction—from within—is exactly the meaning of the Chinese term for "nature," *tzu-jan* or spontaneity.

The form of Christianity differs from the form of nature because in the Church and in its spiritual atmosphere we are in a universe that has been *made*. Outside the Church we are in a universe that has *grown*. Thus the God who made the world stands outside it as the carpenter stands outside his artifacts, but the Tao which grows the world is within it. Christian doctrine admits, in theory, that God is immanent, but in practice it is his transcendence, his otherness, which is always stressed. We are permitted to think of him as within things and within the world only on the strict condition that we maintain an infinite qualitative distance between God and the creature which he inhabits. Even on the inside he is outside, as the architect is still really outside the house which he builds, even when he goes in to decorate the interior.

Conceiving, then, man and the universe as made, the Western and Christian mind endeavors to interpret them mechanically—and this is at once its genius and its blindness. It is an *idée fixe* that the universe consists of distinct things or entities, which are precisely the structural parts of artifacts. Man himself is a part, brought from outside into the total assemblage of nature as a part is added to a building. Furthermore, the workings of the natural universe are understood in terms of logical laws—the mechanical order of things viewed as a linear series of causes and effects, under the limitations of a consciousness which takes them in and symbolizes them one at a time, piece by piece. Earth and sky are measured by approximating the wayward and whimsical shapes of nature to the abstract circles, triangles, and straight lines of Euclid. It appears that nature is a mechanism because such a mentality can grasp only as much of nature as it can fit into some mechanical or mathematical analogy. Thus it never really sees nature. It sees only the pattern of geometrical forms which it has managed to project upon it.

Unhappily, this mechanical cast of thought turns back upon God himself, for although Christianity wants above all to insist that God is personal and living, his nature as conceived in practice lacks the most important attribute of personality. God is actually conceived as a set of principles —principles of morality and reason, of science and art. His love tempered with justice is likewise principled, since it is willed love rather than felt love, the masculine Logos rather than the feminine Eros. The missing attribute is perhaps best called *inwardness*—in the archaic rather than modern and sentimental sense of "having a heart." For as living organisms grow from within outwards, and do not fashion themselves by standing outside themselves like architects or mechanics, they move according to inner spontaneity rather than objective principle. Inwardness is therefore mysterious and inscrutable but not chaotic and capricious. It does not work according to law, but the "laws of nature" are somewhat clumsily abstracted from its behavior—*ex post facto*. They are the mechanical analogy of living and spontaneous order, the triangle standing for the mountain.

Once when my children asked me what God is, I replied that God is the deepest inside of everything. We were eating grapes, and they asked whether God was inside the grapes. When I answered, "Yes," they said, "Let's cut one open and see." Cutting the grape, I said, "That's funny, I don't think we have found the real inside. We've found just another outside. Let's try again." So I cut one of the halves and put the other in one of the children's mouths. "Oh dear," I exclaimed, "we seem to have just some more outsides!" Again I gave one quarter to one of the children and split the other. "Well, all I see is still another outside," I said, eating one eighth part myself. But just as I was about to cut the other, my little girl ran for her bag and cried, "Look! Here is the inside of my bag, but God isn't there." "No," I answered, "that isn't the inside of your bag. That's the inside-outside, but God is the inside-inside, and I don't think we'll ever get at it."

For the truly inward can never become an object. Because of the inwardness of our life-process we do not know, or rather, cannot tell, how or why we live, even though it is our own inmost selves which are doing the living. Yet, in the West at least, we do not actually recognize that we are doing it, for to the extent that we do not consciously control or understand the formation of our nervous systems, we feel that someone or something else—perhaps God—is doing it. We feel strange to our own insides, so that even the mystic feels that his inner experience of God is the experience of something wholly other. But this is because the beat of his heart also feels "other," pulsing with an involuntary life which appears to be its own rather than ours. We have learned to identify ourselves only with the narrow and superficial area of the conscious and the voluntary.

Thus it is in the image of this superficial self that we conceive God, though with its capacities vastly enlarged. God is the "other" conscious Self who designs and operates both our own inner processes and all the workings of nature. By his omniscience he attends consciously to every *thing* at once, and by his omnipotence makes it subject to his will. At first sight this is a fascinating and marvellous conception—an infinitely conscious mind, concentrated simultaneously on every galaxy and every atom with the entirety of its attention. Yet on second thought the conception is more monstrous than marvellous—a kind of intellectual elephantiasis, being simply a colossal magnification and multiplication of the conscious, analytical mode of knowledge. For God is conceived in the image of a severed consciousness, without inwardness, since he knows not only all things but himself as well through and through. He is completely transparent to his own conscious understanding; his subjectivity is totally objective, and for this very reason he lacks an inside. This is perhaps what Western man would himself like to be—a person in total control of himself, analyzed to the ultimate depths of his own unconscious, understood and explained to the last atom of his brain, and to this extent completely mechanized. When every last element of inwardness has become an object of knowledge, the person is, however, reduced to a rattling shell.

Equally monstrous is the notion of absolute omnipotence when considered as perfect self-control, which is actually tantamount to a state of total paralysis. For control is a degree of inhibition, and a system which is perfectly inhibited is completely frozen. Of course, when we say that a pianist or a dancer has perfect control we refer to a certain combination of control and spontaneity. The artist has established an area of control within which he can abandon himself to spontaneity without restraint. We should rather think of God as the one whose spontaneity is so perfect that it needs no control, whose inside is so harmonious that it requires no conscious scrutiny. But this is not the regal God of ecclesiastical imagery, presiding

over a cosmos which is a beneficent despotism run by en-
lightened force.

Fortunately, there is another strain in Christianity,
though it is seen more fully in Eastern Orthodoxy than in
the West. This is the view that the creation is God's
kenosis, or "self-emptying." The incarnation of God the
Son in Jesus is seen as the historical image of the whole
production of the universe.

> Let this mind be in you which was also in Christ Jesus,
> who, being in the form of God, thought not equality with
> God a thing to be grasped, but made himself of no reputa-
> tion, and took upon himself the form of a servant, and was
> made in the likeness of men. And being found in fashion as
> a man, he humbled himself, and became obedient unto
> death.[5]

The world, too, as the creation of God the Son, the Divine
Word, is seen as God's self-abandonment and self-conceal-
ment, so that nature is not so much governed from without
as enlivened from within. The "love which moves the sun
and other stars" is seen as an interior force, which is God
forever giving himself away. There is likewise a strain in
both Catholic and Protestant teaching which regards the
humility and self-abasement of God in Christ as a deeper
revelation of the divine heart than all the imagery of royal
pomp and power. Yet this is offset by the thought that the
"one full, perfect, and sufficient sacrifice" is historically
past, and that now the risen Christ reigns in glory at the
right hand of the Father, whence he shall come to judge
the living and the dead by fire. Again, a subtle theological
insight can reconcile the two motifs. It can see the regal

[5] Philippians 2, 5–8. (Following the AV except in v. 6.) The kenotic
theory of the creation, as distinct from the Incarnation, is perhaps something of a minority view in the Orthodox Church, prevailing mostly
among Hesychast mystics.

imagery as a symbol of the purely inward, spiritual, and unseen glory of humility and love. It can point out that the fire of judgment is the burning pride and anxiety in the hearts of those who will not yield to love and faith. Yet if this be so, the imagery is frankly misleading, and because imagery is far more powerful than rational speech, it would be better to drop it or change it than to explain it away. For it is the imagery rather than the actual doctrine which creates the persuasive feeling of a religion, and to regard it as relatively trivial is merely to be insensitive to the influence which it holds, not only upon those who believe it literally but also upon those who live within its atmosphere—however allegorically they may understand it.[6]

Returning, then, to the personal impression which I mentioned at the start, the imagery of Christianity and the atmosphere of the Church seem utterly foreign to the world beyond its walls. But the reason is that when I leave the Church and the city behind and go out under the sky, when I am with the birds, for all their voraciousness, with the clouds, for all their thunders, and with the oceans, for all their tempests and submerged monsters—I cannot feel Christianly because I am in a world which grows from within. I am simply incapable of feeling its life as coming from above, from beyond the stars, even recognizing this to be a figure of speech. More exactly, I cannot feel that its life comes from Another, from one who is qualitatively

[6] A history of Christian theology and apologetics might be written from the standpoint that their development has arisen largely from the embarrassment of Biblical imagery, and the constant necessity of explaining it away. The writings of the early Fathers, almost as a matter of course, treat much of the Old Testament allegorically in order to rationalize the crude behavior of the Lord God in early Hebrew imagery, which Origen called "puerile." And to this day the apologist has to keep on pointing out that it is not necessary to think of God as a white-haired old gentleman on a throne, nor of heaven as a golden city above the sky.

and spiritually external to all that lives and grows. On the contrary, I feel this whole world to be moved from the inside, and from an inside so deep that it is my inside as well, more truly I than my surface consciousness. My sense of kinship with this world is not only with its obviously sympathetic and beautiful aspects, but also with the horrendous and strange. For I have found that the monstrous and inhuman aspects of fish and insects and reptiles are not so much in them as in me. They are external embodiments of my natural creeps and shudders at the thought of pain and death.

To some extent the conflict between spirit and nature is based on the association of death and decay with evil, as if they were not originally part of the divine plan. It is easy, of course, to show that life is life-death rather than life as opposed to death, but rationalizations do not alter a revulsion so deeply embedded. Yet the problem of death is surely not to be solved by the abolition of death, which is almost analogous to chopping off the head to cure headache. The problem lies in our revulsion, and especially in our unwillingness to feel revulsion—as if it were a weakness of which we should be ashamed.

But, once again, the association of God with being and life to the exclusion of nonbeing and death, and the attempt to triumph over death by the miracle of resurrection, is the failure to see that these pairs are not alternatives but correlatives. To be or not to be is *not* the question, for pure being and pure nonbeing are alike conceptual ghosts. But as soon as the "inner identity" of these correlatives is felt, as well as that which lies between man and nature, the knower and the known, death seems simply to be a return to that unknown inwardness out of which we were born. This is not to say that death, biologically speaking, is reversed birth. It is rather that the truly inward

source of one's life was never born, but has always remained inside, somewhat as the life remains in the tree,
though the fruits may come and go. Outwardly, I am one
apple among many. Inwardly, I am the tree.[7]

Possibly this is what Jesus meant when he said, "I am
the vine; you are the branches." For Christianity is not
necessarily against nature, and within its tradition lie the
seeds of a flowering which may someday change its atmosphere profoundly. The rigid Cross may blossom like
the Rod of Jesse, and among its thorns bear flowers, because, as an ancient hymn suggests, the Cross is really a
tree.

> Crux fidelis, inter omnes
> Arbor una nobilis;
> Nulla silva talem profert
> Fronde, flore, germine.
> Dulce lignum, dulces clavos,
> Dulce pondus sustinet.

Faithful Cross, the one Tree noble above all; no forest
affords the like of this in leaf, or flower, or seed. Sweet the
wood, sweet the nails, and sweet the weight it bears.

This is what must happen if the Chinese artist is to be able
to paint the Crucifixion. Certainly this does not mean the
mere symbolic substitution of a tree for the stiff wooden
beams. Nor does it mean a prettification of the symbol to
conceal the agony and blood. It would simply be the outward sign that Western man had discovered the God of
nature instead of the God of abstraction, and that the
Crucifixion is not just a distant and isolated historical

[7] This is of course speaking poetically—not fancifully but analogically.
Obviously the "life" in the tree is not what we mean when we think of
"life" as related to "death." It is the "inner identity" of the two which
cannot be expressed outwardly because words, as classifiers, restrict us to
talking about classes in which things either are or are not.

event but the inner life of a world, which, when seen from
beyond the narrowly individual point of view, is sacrificial
to its core. For the fact that life is ever related to death,
living by the sacrifice of life, shows only that this "merely
natural" world is the very incarnation of "This is my Body
which is given for you, and this is my Blood which is shed
for you." Prophetically, then, the hymn continues:

> Flecte ramos, arbor alta,
> Tensa laxa viscera,
> Et rigor lentescat ille,
> Quem dedit nativitas;
> Et superni membra Regis
> Tende miti stipite.

Bend thy boughs, O lofty Tree; loosen thy taut sinews,
soften thy native hardness, and upon a gentle stem spread
out the members of the heavenly King.

But the taut sinews have not yet relaxed, and this is because nature is still feared as the beguiler and temptress,
the Spider Mother, the abyss of universal flux which is
always threatening to swallow the human person. Nature
is seen as the wilderness encroaching upon the garden
and the ocean washing away the shore—blind, disorganized, almost cancerous proliferation, against which every
human work must be defended with perpetual vigilance.
Chief of these works is the personality, the conscious ego,
which needs an ark of salvation against the waters of the
unconscious and its vast currents of "animal" lust and fear.

Christian reason as distinct from feeling knows, however, that nature is in process of redemption and that its
dark and destructive aspects work only under the permis-
sion and control of the will of God. Limitless in power,
the divine order is in no danger from nature. But the human order, with its awesome gift of freedom, is secure

against nature only so long as it patterns itself upon the divine. As soon as the human turns away from the divine, nature becomes, like the devils, an instrument of the wrath of God. Thus when a post-Christian technological society sees nature only as a vast randomness upon which man must relentlessly impose his order, the Christian finds himself in a position to point out that nature will always be the enemy to the man who has lost God. He will remind us of the saints who could live unharmed among wild beasts and who had power to command the forces of nature miraculously.

Yet at root this is a conception of universal unity which is an imperium, depending ultimately upon the force of divine omnipotence, a cosmology whose order is political rather than organic. It is true that as Christianity matures the force of omnipotence is seen more and more as the persuasive force of love, just as in well-established states it becomes possible to abolish capital punishment and send criminals to psychiatric hospitals instead of prisons. Yet even in the most beneficent state, force remains the ultimate authority however well hidden. This is because, politically conceived, people are *others*, that is to say, alien wills and isolated consciousnesses upon which order has to be imposed from without.

Political order is, then, different in principle from organic order, wherein the parts constitute a whole by nature as distinct from force or persuasion. In organic order the whole is primary, and the parts arise mutually within it. But in political order the whole is contrived. There is no "body politic" since political societies are put together rather than grown. Similarly, neither the universe nor the Church can be considered the Body of Christ while they are also considered as the Kingdom of God. The two conceptions are profoundly contradictory. There is no common measure between the order of the Vine and the order of the City. But, once again, it is clear that a political conception of the universe and, furthermore, a political conception of human society go hand in hand with a fractured and disorganized view of the world, with a mentality so fascinated by speech and thought that it has lost the power to feel the interval, the reality lying between terms. The terms, the Euclidean points, ends, and boundaries, are everything and the content nothing.

2: Science and Nature

A KING OF ANCIENT INDIA, OPPRESSED BY the roughness of the earth upon soft human feet, proposed that his whole territory should be carpeted with skins. However, one of his wise men pointed out that the same result could be achieved far more simply by taking a single skin and cutting off small pieces to bind beneath the feet. These were the first sandals. To a Hindu the point of this story is not its obvious illustration of technical ingenuity. It is a parable of two different attitudes to the world, attitudes which correspond approximately to those of the progressive and traditional types of culture. Only in this case the more technically skillful solution represents the traditional culture, in which it is felt that it is easier for man to adapt himself to nature than to adapt nature to himself. This is why science and technology, as we know them, did not arise in Asia.

Westerners generally feel that Asian indifference to the technical control of nature is either tropical laziness or the lack of a social conscience. It is easy to believe that religions which concern themselves with inward rather than outward solutions to suffering encourage callousness toward hunger, injustice, and disease. It is easy to say that they are aristocrats' methods of exploiting the poor. But it is, perhaps, not so easy to see that the poor are also being exploited when they are persuaded to desire more and more possessions, and led to confuse happiness with progressive acquisition. The power to change nature or to

perform miracles conceals the truth that suffering is relative, and that the fact that nature abhors a vacuum is
above all true of troubles.

The Western experiment in changing the face of nature
by science and technology has its roots in the political
cosmology of Christianity. For Christian apologists are
indeed justified in pointing out that science has arisen pre-
eminently in the context of the Hebrew-Christian tradition,
notwithstanding the constant conflicts between the two.
There can be conflict between Christianity and science for
the very reason that both are speaking the same language
and dealing with the same universe—the universe of facts.
The claim of Christianity to be unique is bound up with
its insistence on the truth of certain historical facts. To
other spiritual traditions historical facts are of minor
importance, but to Christianity it has always been "of the
essence" that Jesus Christ did in fact rise physically from
the dead, that he was, biologically speaking, born of a virgin, and that even God has the kind of objective and in-
tractable reality which we associate with "hard facts."
The Christian who does not feel this to be so will also
insist less upon the uniqueness of his religion. However,
the temper of most current theology, both Catholic and
Protestant, is to re-emphasize the historicity of the Biblical
narrative. Even among theological liberals who have their
doubts about miracles, this trend takes the curious form
of arguing that the historical and narrative style of Christianity, however unhistorical in certain respects, nevertheless reveals that history is the unfolding of God's purposes.

Christianity is also unique in that the historical facts
upon which it insists are miracles, betokening a state of
mind for which the transformation of the physical world
is of immense importance, for "if Christ be not risen from
the dead, then is your faith vain." Other traditions contain

miraculous elements aplenty, but they are always treated
as incidental signs, corroborating the divine authority of
the performer. They are never the heart of the matter. But
nothing is more important for Christianity than the sub-
servience of nature to the commands of Christ, culminat-
ing in his victory over the hardest and most certain of all
natural facts—death itself.

However post-Christian and secular the present culture
of the West may seem to be, it is still the culture uniquely
preoccupied with miracles—that is to say, with the transformation of that world which is felt to be objective and
external to the ego. Concurrently, an unparalleled cultural
imperialism has taken the place of religious proselytism,
and the progressive course of history toward the establish-
ment of the Kingdom of God is seen in terms of the expansion of technological power, the increasing "spiritual-
ization" of the physical world through the abolition of its
finite limitations.

All this has its roots in the political cosmology of the
Hebrew-Christian tradition, which, until very recently,
was also the cosmology of Western science and in some
respects still remains so. For, as we have seen, a political
universe is one in which separate things, facts, and events
are governed by the force of law. However much ideas of
the laws of nature may have changed, there is no doubt
that the idea of natural law first arose from the supposition
that the world obeyed the commandments of a ruler conceived in the image of an earthly king.

Yet the notion of natural law is not fully accounted for
by a primitive analogy between the world and a political
kingship. There must also be taken into consideration a
mode of thought apart from which such an analogy would
hardly suggest itself. So far as one can see, this mode of
thought arises from an accidental confusion which could

easily occur in the development of language in particular and of abstract thought in general.

It is commonly felt that the mind can think only of one thing at a time, and language, in so far as it is the main instrument of thought, confirms this impression by being a linear series of signs read or sounded one at a time. The sense of this common feeling is presumably that conscious thought is focused attention, and that such concentration of our awareness is difficult or impossible when the field of attention is too complex. Attention therefore requires selection. The field of awareness must be divided into relatively simple unities or wholes, so structured that their parts can be taken in at one glance. This may be done both by breaking the whole field down into component parts of the required simplicity, and by so screening out certain details of the whole that it is reduced to a single easily comprehensible form. It is thus that we actually see or hear infinitely more than we attend to or think about, and although we respond and adjust ourselves with extraordinary intelligence to much that we never notice, we feel in better control of a situation to the degree that we can bring it under conscious scrutiny.

Now the simplified units of attention thus selected from the total field of awareness are what we call things and events, or facts. This does not ordinarily occur to us because we naïvely suppose that things are what we see in the first place, prior to the act of conscious attention. Obviously the eye as such does not see things: it sees the total visual field in all its infinite detail. Things appear to the mind when, by conscious attention, the field is broken down into easily thinkable unities. Yet we tend to consider this an act of discovery. Studying the visual or tactile field, intelligence arrives at the conclusion that there are actually things in the external world—a conclusion which appears to be verified by acting upon that assumption. This is to say, in other words, that by attending to the sensed world with the aid of these concentrated and simplified "grasps" or "glances" of the mind, we are able to predict its behavior and find our way around it.

Yet the conclusion does not actually follow. We are also able to predict events and manage the external world by breaking down distances into feet and inches, weights into pounds and ounces, and motions into minutes and seconds. But do we actually suppose that twelve inches of wood are twelve separate bits of wood? We do not. We know that "breaking" wood into inches or pounds is done abstractly and not concretely. It is not, however, so easy to see that breaking the field of awareness into things and events is also done abstractly, and that things are the measuring units of thought just as pounds are the measuring units of weighing. But this begins to be apparent when we realize that any one thing may, by analysis, be broken down into any number of component things, or may in its turn be regarded as the component part of some larger thing.

The real difficulty of understanding this point is that whereas inches are divisions on a ruler which do not themselves appear on the wooden board to be measured, the delineation of things seems to follow divisions and boundaries actually given in nature. For example, the thing called the human body is divided from other things in its environment by the clearly discernible surface of the skin. The point, though, is that the skin *divides* the body from the rest of the world as one thing from others in thought but not in nature. In nature the skin is as much a joiner as a divider, being, as it were, the bridge whereby the inner organs have contact with air, warmth, and light.

Just because concentrated attention is exclusive, selec-

tive, and divisive it is much easier for it to notice differences than unities. Visual attention notices things as figures against a contrasting background, and our thought
about such things emphasizes the difference between figure and ground. The outline of the figure or the "inline"
of the ground divides the two from each other. Yet we do
not so easily notice the union or inseparability of figure
and ground, or solid and space. This is easily seen when
we ask what would become of the figure or the solid without any surrounding ground or space. Conversely, we
might ask what would become of the surrounding space
if unoccupied by any solids. The answer is surely that it
would no longer be space, for space is a "surrounding function" and there would be nothing to surround. It is important to note that this mutuality or inseparability of figure and ground is not only logical and grammatical but
also sensuous.[1]

Figure-and-ground, then, constitute a relationship—an
inseparable relationship of unity-in-diversity. But when
human beings become preoccupied with concentrated attentiveness, with a type of thought which is analytic, divisive, and selective, they cease to notice the mutuality of
contrasting "things" and the "identity" of differences. Similarly, when we ask what we really mean by a fact or a
thing, we realize that because facts are divisions or selec-
tions of experience there can never be less than two! One
solitary fact or thing cannot exist by itself, since it would
be infinite—without delineating limits, without anything
other. Now this essential duality and multiplicity of facts
should be the clearest evidence of their interdependence
and inseparability.

[1] The naïve idea that there is first of all empty space and then things
filling it underlies the classical problem of how the world came out of
nothing. Now the problem has to be rephrased, "How did something-
and-nothing come out of . . . what?"

What it comes to, then, is that the fundamental realities of nature are not, as thought construes them, separate things. The world is not a collection of objects assembled or added together so as to *come* into relationship with each other. The fundamental realities are the relations or "fields of force" in which facts are the terms or limits—somewhat as hot and cold are the upper and lower terms (that is, termini or ends) of the field of temperature, and scalp and soles the upper and lower limits of the body. Scalp and soles are obviously surfaces *of* the body, and though a person may be scalped, a scalp is never found *sui generis*, coming into being all on its own. But, save through the use of rather unsatisfactory analogies, words and thought forms cannot embrace this world. "Relations" rather than "things" as the basic constituents of nature sound impossibly tenuous and abstract, unless it can dawn upon us that relations are what we are actually sensing and feeling. We know nothing more concrete.

But the dawning of this realization becomes still more remote when we proceed from the primary act of abstraction, selective attention, to the secondary, the signifying of thoughts with words. Because words other than proper names are classifiers, they will aggravate the impression that the world is a disjointed multiplicity. For when we say *what* anything is we identify it with a class. There is no other way of saying what this or that is than to classify it. But that is simply to divide it from everything else, to stress its differentiating characteristics as the most important. Thus it comes to be felt that an identity is a matter of separation, that, for instance, my identity is firstly in my role or class, and secondly in the special ways in which I differ from other members of my class. If, then, I am identified by my differences, my boundaries, my divisions from all else, I experience selfhood as a sense of separation. Thereupon I fail to notice, to feel identified with, the concrete unity which underlies these selected and abstracted marks of difference. Marks of difference are then felt as forms of separation and dissociation rather than relationship. In this situation I feel the world as something to which I must *form* a relation rather than with which I *have* a relation.

A political cosmology presupposes, then, this fractured way of experiencing the world. God is not, as in Hindu cosmology, the underlying identity of the differences, but one of the differences—albeit the ruling difference. Man is related to God as to another distinct person, as subject to king or as son to father. The individual is, from the beginning and out of nothing, created separate and must bring himself or be brought into conformity with the divine will.

Furthermore, because the world consists of things, and because things are defined by their classes, and their classes are ordered and marked by words, it appears that Logos, that word-and-thought actually *underlies* the world. "And God *said*, Let there be light." "By the word of the Lord were the heavens made, and all the hosts of them by the breath of his mouth." When it is not recognized that thought orders the world, it is supposed that thought discovers an order which is already there—a type of order which is, furthermore, expressible in terms of word-and-thought.

Here, then, is the genesis of two of the most important historical premises of Western science. The first is that there is a law of nature, an order of things and events awaiting our discover and that this order can be formulated in thought, that is, in words or in some type of notation. The second is that the law of nature is universal, a premise deriving from monotheism, from the idea of one God ruling the whole world.

Science is, moreover, an extreme instance of the entire method of attention which we have been discussing. It is an awareness of nature based upon the selective, analytic, and abstractive way of focusing attention. It understands the world by reducing it as minutely as possible to intelligible things. This it does by a "universal calculus," that is, by translating the formlessness of nature into structures made up of simple and manageable units, as a surveyor measures a "shapeless" piece of land by approximating its areas as minutely as possible to such simple abstract figures as triangles, squares, and circles. By this method all oddities and irregularities are progressively screened out until at last it appears that God himself is the supreme geometer. We say, "How astonishing it is that natural structures conform so precisely to geometrical laws!"— forgetting that by ignoring their irregularities we have forced them to do so. But this we have been able to do by analysis, by the ever minuter division of the world into parts which approximate the supreme simplicity of mathematical points.

Alternatively, this way of regularizing the world may be illustrated by the method of the matrix. Superimpose a transparent sheet of finely squared graph paper upon some complex natural image. The "formless" image can then be described with approximate precision in terms of the highly formal arrangement of squares. Seen through such a screen, the path of an object moving at random can be "plotted" in terms of so many squares up or down, left or right. Reduced to these terms, we can by statistical averages predict the approximate trend of its future motion— and then suppose that the object itself is *obeying* statistical laws. The object, however, is doing nothing of the kind. The statistical laws are being "obeyed" by our regularized model of the object's behavior.

In the twentieth century scientists are increasingly aware of the fact that the laws of nature are not discovered but invented, and the whole notion that nature is obeying or following some innate pattern or order is being supplanted by the idea that these patterns are not determinative but descriptive. This is a fundamental revolution in the philosophy of science which has hardly reached the general public and which has still but barely affected some of the special sciences. The scientist was first discovering the laws of God, in the faith that the workings of the world could be reformulated into the terms of the word, the reason, and the law which they were obeying. As the hypothesis of God made no difference to the accuracy of his predictions, he began to leave it out and to consider the world as a machine, something which followed laws with no lawgiver. Lastly, the hypothesis of pre-existing and determinative laws became unnecessary. They were seen simply as human tools, like knives, with which nature is chopped up into digestible portions.

There are signs, however, that this is but one phase of a still more radical change in the outlook of science. For we may ask whether scientific method must confine itself to the analytic and abstractive mode of attention in studying nature. Until not so long ago the main preoccupation of almost every scientific discipline was classification—a minute, rigorous, and exhaustive identification of species, whether of birds or fish, chemicals or bacilli, organs or diseases, crystals or stars. Obviously this approach encouraged an atomistic and disintegrated view of nature, the disadvantages of which begin to appear when, on the basis of this view, science becomes technology and men start to extend their control of the world. For they begin to discover that nature cannot wisely be controlled in the same way in which it has been studied—piecemeal. Nature is through and through relational, and interference at one point has interminable and unforeseeable effects. The analytic study of these interrelations produces an ever-growing accumulation of extremely complicated information, so vast and so complex as to be unwieldy for many practical purposes, especially when quick decisions are needed.

Consequently the progress of technology begins to have the opposite of its intended effect. Instead of simplifying human tasks, it makes them more complicated. No one dares move without consulting an expert. The expert in his turn cannot hope to have mastered more than a small section of the ceaselessly expanding volume of information. But whereas formal scientific knowledge is departmentalized, the world is not, so that the mastery of a single department of knowledge is often as frustrating as a closetful of left shoes. This is not only a problem of dealing with such formally "scientific" questions as endocrinology, soil chemistry, or nuclear fall-out. In a society whose means of production and communication are highly technological, the most ordinary matters of politics, economics, and law become so involved that the individual citizen feels paralyzed. The growth of bureaucracy and totalitarianism has, then, far less to do with sinister influences than with the mere mechanics of control in an impossibly complex system of interrelations.

Yet if this were the whole story scientific knowledge would already have reached the point of total self-strangulation. That it has done so only in some degree is because the scientist actually understands interrelations by other means than analysis and step-by-step thinking. In practice he relies heavily upon intuition—upon a process of intelli-

gence whose steps are unconscious, which does not appear
to work in the painfully linear, one-thing-at-a-time fashion
of thought, and which can therefore grasp whole fields of
related detail simultaneously.

For the notion that the interrelatedness of nature is
complex and highly detailed is merely the result of translating it into the linear units of thought. Despite its rigor
and despite its initial successes, this is an extremely clumsy
mode of intelligence. Just as it is a highly complicated
task to drink water with a fork instead of a glass, so the
complexity of nature is not innate but a consequence of
the instruments used to handle it. There is nothing complex about walking, breathing, and circulating one's blood.
Living organisms have developed these functions without thinking about them at all. The circulation of the blood
becomes complex only when stated in physiological terms,
that is, when understood by means of a conceptual model
constructed of the kind of simple units which conscious
attention requires. The natural world seems a marvel of
complexity, requiring a vastly intricate intelligence to
create and govern it, just because we have represented it
to ourselves in the clumsy "notation" of thought. In a
somewhat similar way, multiplication and division are
processes of the most frustrating complexity for those
working with Roman or Egyptian numerals. But with Ara-
bic numerals they are relatively simple, and with an
abacus simpler still.

Understanding nature by means of thought is like trying to make out the contours of an enormous cave with
the aid of a small flashlight casting a bright but very thin
beam. The path of the light and the series of "spots" over
which it has passed must be retained in memory, and from
this record the general appearance of the cave must laboriously be reconstructed.

In practice, then, the scientist must perforce use his intuition for grasping the wholes of nature, though he does not trust it. He must always stop to check intuitive insight with the thin bright beam of analytic thought. For intuition can so easily be wrong, just as the "organic intelligence" which regulates the body without thought cannot always be relied upon to avoid the "mistakes" of congenital deformity or cancer, nor to control instincts which, under special circumstances, lead directly to destruction. Thus it is natural enough and "healthy" enough to want to reproduce the species, but the reproductive urge cannot be relied upon to keep a watch on the environment and automatically check itself when the food supply is insufficient. Hence the only way of correcting the errors of intuition or unconscious intelligence seems to be by the laborious work of analysis and experiment. But this involves an interference with the natural order from the start, and the wisdom of this interference cannot be known until its work is well advanced!

Therefore the scientist has to ask himself whether the "mistakes" of nature are really mistakes. Does a species destroy itself in the interests of the natural order as a whole—in the sense that if it did not do so, life would be intolerable for all, including itself? Are "errors" of congenital disease, or of epidemics or pestilence, necessary for maintaining a balance of life? Will correction of these errors give rise in the long run to far more serious problems than one has solved? And will the solution of *those* problems in turn create ever more fantastic difficulties? Must unconscious intelligence every so often be wrong lest, if it were always right, the species would be too successful and again upset the balance?

On the other hand, he may ask whether the birth of conscious analysis is not itself an act of unconscious intelligence. Is conscious interference with nature actually quite natural, in the sense that it is still working in the interests of the natural order as a whole, even if it is going to involve the elimination of man? Or may it be that in pushing conscious analysis just as far as we can we shall discover means of enabling the unconscious intelligence to be far more effective?

The difficulty with all these questions is that we can hardly find out the answers until it is too late to make use of them. What, furthermore, will be the test of doing the right thing? What, in other words, is the "good" of the natural order as a whole? The usual answer to the problem of what is good for any or all species is simply survival. Science is mainly interested in prediction because it assumes that the chief good of humanity is to continue into the future. This is likewise the test of almost all practical action: it has "survival-value." Accepting this premise, that the good of life lies in its indefinite perpetuation through time, and assuming that such perpetuation must be pleasant for it to go on at all, the test of whether we have done wisely is that we are still here, and seem likely to remain for as long as we can foresee.

But on this assumption the human race had survived, and seemed likely to go on surviving, for perhaps more than a million years before the arrival of modern technology. We must, on this premise, assume that it had acted wisely thus far. We may argue that its life was not highly pleasant, but it is difficult to know what this means. The race was certainly pleased to go on living, for it did so. On the other hand, after a bare two centuries of industrial technology the prospects of human survival are being quite seriously questioned. It is not unlikely that we may eat or blow ourselves off the planet.

Yet surely the ideal of survival is completely inane.

Studying human and animal psychology, it does indeed seem that "self-preservation is the first law of nature," though it is possible that this is an anthropomorphism, a projection into nature of a peculiarly human attitude. If survival is the test of wisdom, the significance of life is merely time: we go on in order to keep going on. Our attitude to experience seems to be one of perpetual hunger, for even when we are satisfied and delighted to be alive we keep calling for more. The cry "Encore!" is the highest mark of approval. Obviously, this is because no moment of life is a true fulfillment. Even in satisfaction there remains a gnawing emptiness which nothing save an infinity of time can fill, for "all joys want eternity."

But the hunger for time is the direct result of our specialization in narrowed attention, of the mode of consciousness which takes the world in serially, one thought and one thing at a time. Each experience is for this reason partial, fractured, and incomplete, and no amount of these fragments ever add up to a whole experience, a true fulfillment. By and large they attain only to the weariness of satiation. The impression that all nature, like ourselves, hungers endlessly for survival is, then, the necessary result of the way in which we study it. The answer is predetermined by the character of the question. Nature seems to be a series of unsatisfactory moments ever demanding more because those are the terms in which we perceive it. We understand it by cutting it to pieces, assume that it is in itself this heap of fragments, and conclude that it is a system of endless incompleteness which can seek fulfillment only through everlasting addition.

Thought and science are therefore raising problems which their terms of study can never answer, many of which are doubtless problems only for thought. The trisection of an angle is similarly an insoluble problem only for compass and straight-edge construction, and Achilles cannot overtake the tortoise so long as their progress is considered piecemeal, endlessly halving the distance between them. However, as it is not Achilles but the method of measurement which fails to catch up with the tortoise, so it is not man but his method of thought which fails to find fulfillment in experience. This is by no means to say that science and analytic thought are useless and destructive tools, but rather that the people who use them must be greater than their tools. To be an effective scientist one must be more than a scientist, and a philosopher must be more than a thinker. For the analytic measurement of nature tells us nothing if we cannot see nature in any other way.

Thus the scientist *as* scientist does not see nature at all—or rather he sees it only by means of an instrument of measurement, as if trees became visible to the carpenter only as he sawed them into planks or marked them out with his ruler. More importantly, man as ego does not see nature at all. For man as ego is man identifying himself or his mind, his total awareness, with the narrowed and exclusive style of attention which we call consciousness.[2] Thus the radical change which may yet overcome modern science will be the recognition of itself as a secondary form of perception, related to a primary and more basic form. This involves a good deal more than the scientist's recognition that there are other modes of knowledge than his own—for example, the religious—all of which are valid in their own spheres. For this merely puts the scientist as a man of religion in one compartment, and the scientist

---

[2] Trigant Burrow (1) coined the useful terms "ditention" and "cotention" for the intensive and extensive modes of awareness. His whole discussion of the relation between the psychoneuroses and ditentive thought and feeling is most provocative.

as scientist in another. But we have seen that the most important scientific insights, or intuitions, come precisely through the somewhat reluctant use of a nonthinking mode of awareness.

It is therefore becoming generally realized that for the most creative research, men of science must be trusted and encouraged to let their minds wander unsystematically without any pressure for results. The visitor to such an inspired foundation as the Institute for Advanced Studies at Princeton will see some of the world's greatest mathematicians just sitting at their desks with their heads in their hands, or staring blankly out of the window, apparently financed munificently to do nothing but "goof off." Yet as R. G. H. Siu has shown in his *Tao of Science*, this is precisely the Taoist principle of "using no-knowledge to attain knowledge," the Western discovery of the creative power of *wu-nien*, or "no-thought," and *kuan*, or contemplation without strained attention. As an experienced director of research he has cogently argued that such a mode of awareness is essential when research is expected to bring forth new concepts, and to be something more than the verification of old ones.[3] At present this mode is mistrusted and rigorously checked by analysis, but it is highly possible that the unreliability of scientific intuition is due to lack of use, and to the constant distraction of the mind by selective attention both in scientific and everyday consciousness.

Now the recovery of our extensive and inclusive type of awareness is completely different from the acquisition of a

[3] The whole work, Siu (1), may be read as an expansion of themes discussed in the present chapter. Unfortunately, it did not come to my attention until I had almost finished writing this book. It gives a very wide application of Chinese thought to the problems of science, though for the Western reader it is rather too vague in describing the character of the necessary mental attitude.

moral virtue, to be urged upon society by persuasion and propaganda and cultivated by discipline and practice. As we know, such idealisms are notorious for their failure. Furthermore, moral and spiritual idealisms with all their efforts and disciplines aimed at the future are forms of the very mode of awareness which is giving us the trouble. For they perceive good and bad, ideal and real, separatively and fail to see that "goodness" is necessarily a "bad" man's ideal, that courage is the goal of cowards, and that peace is sought only by the disturbed. As Lao-tzu put it:

> When the great Tao is lost,
> we have "human-heartedness" and "righteousness."
> When "wisdom" and "sagacity" are ,
> we have great hypocrites.
> When the six family relations are not in harmony,
> we have "filial devotion."
> When the nation is confused and disordered,
> we have "loyal ministers." xviii

As "you cannot make a silk purse from a sow's ear," no amount of effort will turn turmoil into peace. For, as another Taoist saying puts it, "When the wrong man uses the right means, the right means work in the wrong way."

Thought, with its serial, one-at-a-time way of looking at things, is ever looking to the future to solve problems which can be handled only in the present—but not in the fragmentary present of fixed and pointed attention. The solution has to be found, as Krishnamurti has said, in the problem and not away from it. In other words, the "bad" man's disturbing emotions and urgent desires have to be seen as they are—or, better, the moment in which they arise has to be seen as it is, without narrowing attention upon any aspect of it. And just here, instead of straining toward a future in which one hopes to be different, the mind opens and admits a whole experience in which and by which the problem of what is the "good" of life is answered. In the words of Goethe's *Fragment on Nature:*

> At each moment she starts upon a long, long journey and at each moment reaches her end. . . . All is eternally present in her, for she knows neither past nor future. For her the present is eternity.

3: The Art of Feeling

THE WORDS WHICH ONE MIGHT BE TEMPTED
to use for a silent and wide-open mind are mostly terms of
abuse—thoughtless, mindless, unthinking, empty-headed,
and vague. Perhaps this is some measure of an innate fear
of releasing the chronic cramp of consciousness by which
we grasp the facts of life and manage the world. It is only
to be expected that the idea of an awareness which is
something other than sharp and selective fills us with considerable disquiet. We are perfectly sure that it would
mean going back to the supposedly confused sensitivity of
infants and animals, that we should be unable to distinguish up from down, and that we should certainly be run
over by a car the first time we went out on the street.

Narrowed, serial consciousness, the memory-stored
stream of impressions, is the means by which we have the
sense of ego. It enables us to feel that behind thought
there is a thinker and behind knowledge a knower—an
individual who stands aside from the changing panorama
of experience to order and control it as best he may. If
the ego were to disappear, or rather, to be seen as a useful
fiction, there would no longer be the duality of subject and
object, experiencer and experience. There would simply be
a continuous, self-moving stream of experiencing, without
the sense either of an active subject who controls it or of
a passive subject who suffers it. The thinker would be
seen to be no more than the series of thoughts, and the

feeler no more than the feelings. As Hume said in the *Treatise of Human Nature:*

> For my part, when I enter most intimately into what I call *myself*, I always stumble on some particular perception or other, of heat or cold, light or shade, love or hatred, pain or pleasure. I never can catch *myself* at any time without a perception, and never can observe any thing but the perception. . . . [We are] nothing but a bundle or collection of different perceptions, which succeed each other with an inconceivable rapidity, and are in a perpetual flux and movement.[1]

Now this is just what we fear—the loss of human identity and integrity in a transient stream of atoms. Hume, arguing against the notion of the self as a metaphysical or mental substance, had of course no alternative conception other than the "bundle or collection" of intrinsically separate perceptions, for he was translating his experience into the disjointed terms of linear thought. He maintained that all our impressions are "different, and distinguishable, and separable from each other, and may be separately consider'd, and may exist separately, and have no need of any thing to support their existence." Having seen the fiction of the separate ego-substance, he failed to see the fiction of separate things or perceptions which the ego, as a mode of awareness, abstracts from nature. As we have seen, inherently separate things can be ordered only mechanically or politically, so that without a real ego in which impressions are integrated and ordered, human experience is delivered over to mechanism or chaos.

If the world of nature is neither things seen by an ego nor things, some of which are sensations, bundled mechanically together, but a field of "organic" relations,

[1] Hume (1), p. 252.

there is no need to fear that disorder is the only alternative
to political order or to mechanism. The stream of human
experience would then be ordered neither by a transcendental ego nor by a transcendental God but by itself.
Yet this is what we usually mean by a mechanical or automatic order, since the machine is what "goes by itself." We
have seen, however, that there is a profound difference of
operation betwen organism and mechanism. An organism
can be represented in terms of a mechanical model just as
"formless" shapes can be approximated by geometric
models and as the movements of the stars can be translated
into the figures in an almanac. But as the celestial bodies
are other than and infinitely more than numerical relations
and schedules, organisms and natural forms must never
be confused with their mechanical representations.

Once again, because the order of thought is a linear,
bit-by-bit series, it can approximate but never comprehend
a system of relations in which everything is happening
simultaneously. It would be as if our narrowed consciousness had to take charge of all the operations of the body
so that, unless it took thought of them, the glands and
nerves and arteries could not do their work. As language,
both written and spoken, so eloquently shows, the order of
thought must be strung out in a line. But nature is not
strung out in a line. Nature is, at the very least, a volume,
and at most an infinitely dimensioned field. We need, then,
another conception of natural order than the logical, than
the order of the Logos or word based on bit-by-bit awareness.

As Needham has shown, Chinese philosophy provides
this in the Neo-Confucian (and Buddhist) conception of
li, for which there has been no better English equivalent
than "principle." *Li* is the universal principle of order, but

in this case the principle or principles cannot be stated in terms of law (*tse*). The root meaning of *li* is the markings in jade, the grain in wood, or the fiber in muscle. The root meaning of *tse* is the writing of imperial laws upon sacrificial caldrons.[2] Now the markings in jade are "formless." That is to say, they are unsymmetrical, fluid, and intricate patterns which appeal highly to the Chinese sense of beauty. Thus when it is said that the Tao has "no shape"[3] we are not to imagine a uniform blank so much as a pattern without clearly discernible features, in other words, just exactly what the Chinese painter admires in rocks and clouds, and what he sometimes conveys in the texture of black ink applied with bold strokes of a rather dry brush. In the words of the *Huai Nan Tzu:*

> The Tao of Heaven operates mysteriously and secretly; it has no fixed shape; it follows no definite rules (*tse*); it is so great that you can never come to the end of it; it is so deep that you can never fathom it.[4]

At the same time the order of the Tao is not so inscrutable that man can see it only as confusion. When the artist handles his material, perfection consists in knowing how to follow its nature, how to follow the grain in carving wood, and how to employ the sound-textures of various musical instruments. The nature of the material is precisely *li*. He discovers it, however, not by logical analysis but by *kuan*,[5] to which we have already referred as "silent

---

[2] For the characters see Mathews' *Chinese-English Dictionary* 3864 (*li*) and 6746 (*tse*). For the original forms, see Karlgren's *Grammata Serica* 978 and 906. Since the Romanized forms of Chinese words give little clue to the actual written term, we shall hereinafter identify Chinese terms with their numbers in the Mathews *Dictionary*, e.g., M 3864.
[3] Yung, M 7560.
[4] *Huai Nan Tzu*, 9. Tr. Needham (1), vol. 2, p. 561.
[5] M 3575.

contemplation," or looking at nature without *thinking* in the sense of narrowed attention. Speaking of the hexagram *kuan* in the *Book of Changes*, Wang Pi writes:

> The general meaning of the *tao* of "Kuan" is that one should not govern by means of punishments and legal pressure, but by looking forth one should exert one's influence so as to change all things. Spiritual power can no man see. We do not see Heaven command the four seasons, and yet they never swerve from their course. So also we do not see the sage ordering people about, and yet they obey and spontaneously serve him.[6]

The point is that things are brought into order through regarding them from a viewpoint unrestricted by the ego, since their *li* or pattern cannot be observed while looking and thinking piecemeal, nor when regarding them as objects apart from oneself, the subject. The Chinese character for *kuan* shows the radical sign for "seeing" beside a bird which is probably a heron, and although Needham feels that it may originally have had something to do with watching the flight of birds for omens, I am inclined to think that the root idea was taken from the way in which a heron stands stock-still at the edge of a pool, gazing into the water. It does not seem to be looking *for* fish, and yet the moment a fish moves it dives. *Kuan* is, then, simply to observe silently, openly, and without seeking any particular result. It signifies a mode of observation in which there is no duality of seer and seen: there is simply the seeing. Watching thus, the heron is all pool.

In some respects this is what we mean by *feeling*, as when one learns to dance by watching and "getting the feel of it" rather than following a diagram of the steps. Similarly the bowler in cricket or the pitcher in baseball

[6] Tr. Needham (1), vol. 2, pp. 561–62.

develops his skill by "feel" rather than by studying precise technical directions. So, too, it is by feeling that the musician distinguishes the styles of composers, that the wine taster identifies vintages, that the painter determines compositional proportions, that the farmer foretells the weather, and that the potter throws and shapes his clay. Up to a point these arts have communicable rules, but there is always something indefinable which distinguishes true mastery. As the wheelwright says in the *Chuang-tzu:*

> Let me take an illustration from my own trade. In making a wheel, if you work too slowly, you can't make it firm; if you work too fast, the spokes won't fit in. You must go neither too slowly nor too fast. There must be co-ordination of mind and hand. Words cannot explain what it is, but there is some mysterious art herein. I cannot teach it to my son; nor can he learn it from me. Consequently, though seventy years of age, I am still making wheels in my old age.[7]

Analytically studied, these skills appear at first sight to be the result of "unconscious thinking," the brain acting as an extremely complex electronic computer which delivers its results to the consciousness. In other words, they are the consequence of a thinking process which differs merely in quantity from conscious thought: it is faster and more complex. But this tells us not so much about what the brain does as about the way in which it has been studied and the model to which it has been approximated. The brain may be represented in terms of quantitative measurement, but it does not follow that it works in these terms. On the contrary, it does not work in terms at all, and for this reason can respond intelligently to relations which can be termed only approximately, slowly, and laboriously.

[7] H. A. Giles (1), p. 171.

But if we pursue the question, "How, then, does feeling work?" recognizing that an answer in terms is no answer, we shall have to say that it works as it feels from the inside, in the same way that we feel how to move our legs. We easily forget that this is a more intimate knowledge of our nature than objective description, which is of necessity superficial, being knowledge of surfaces. Thus it is of relatively little use to the scientist to know, in terms, how his brain operates, for in practice he gets his best results when he resorts to feeling or intuition, when his research is a kind of puttering without any specific result in mind. He must, of course, have a knowledge of terms which will enable him to recognize a result when he sees it. But these enable him to communicate the result to himself and to others; they do not supply the result any more than the dictionary and the rules of prosody supply the poet with poetry. *Kuan* as feeling without seeking, or open awareness, is therefore as essential to the scientist, for all his analytic rigor, as to the poet. The attitude is marvellously described by Lin Ching-hsi in his *Poetical Remains of the Old Gentleman of Chi Mountain* as follows:

> Scholars of old time said that the mind is originally empty, and only because of this can it respond [resonate] [8] to natural things without prejudices (lit. traces, *chi*,[9] left behind to influence later vision). Only the empty mind can respond to the things of Nature. Though everything resonates with the mind, the mind should be as if it had never resonated, and things should not remain in it. But once the mind has received (impressions of) natural things, they

[8] *Ying*, M 7477. Needham points out that this is the technical term for "resonance," an idea basic to the Chinese philosophy of the relations between events, derived from the *Book of Changes*. Cf. Eckhart, "If my eye is to discern color, it must itself be free from color."
[9] *M* 502. Also "effects" or "searching out."

tend to remain and not to disappear, thus leaving traces in the mind. It should be like a river gorge with swans flying overhead; the river has no desire to retain the swan, yet the swan's passage is traced out by its shadow without any omission. Take another example. All things, whether beautiful or ugly, are reflected perfectly in a mirror; it never refuses to show anything, nor retains anything afterwards.[10]

Kuan is no more a mind that is merely empty than li, the pattern of the Tao, is a featureless blank. Indeed, kuan is not so much a mind empty of contents as a mind empty of mind. It is mind or "experiencing" at work without the sense of the seeking and staring subject, for the sensation of the ego is the sensation of a kind of effort of consciousness, of a confusion of nerves with muscles. But as glaring and staring do not clarify the eyesight, and as straining to hear does not sharpen the ears, mental "trying" does not enhance understanding. Nevertheless the mind is constantly making efforts to fight off the sense of boredom or depression, to stop being afraid, to get the most out of a pleasure, or to compel itself to be loving, attentive, patient, or happy. On being told that this is wrong, the mind will even make efforts not to make efforts. This can come to an end only as it is clearly seen that all these efforts are as futile as trying to leap into the air and fly, as struggling to sleep, or as forcing an erection of the sexual member. Everyone is familiar with the contradiction of trying to recollect a forgotten name, and though it happens again and again, we never seem to trust the memory to supply the information spontaneously. Yet this is one of the most common forms of what is known in Zen Buddhism as satori —the effortless, spontaneous, and sudden dawning of a

[10] Chi Shan Chi, 4. Tr. Needham (1), vol. 2, p. 89.

realization. The difficulty is of course that the mind strains itself by force of habit, and that until it loses the habit it must be watched—gently—all the time.[11]

In saying that the ego is a sensation of mental strain, we must not overlook the fact that the words "ego" and "I" are sometimes used simply to denote *this* organism as distinct from its soul or from one of its psychological functions. In this sense, of course, "I" does not necessarily denote a state of strain or a psychological excrescence. But the sensation of the ego as a part function of the whole organism, or rather, as an inner entity which owns and inhabits the organism, is the result of an excess of activity in the use of the senses and of certain muscles. This is the habit of using more energy than is necessary to think, see, hear, or make decisions. Thus even when lying flat on the floor most people will continue to make totally needless muscular efforts to retain their position, almost as if they were afraid of the organism losing its shape and dissolving into a jelly. All this arises from anxiety acquired in learning control and co-ordination, for under social pressure

[11] The habitual straining of the mind can be relaxed temporarily by the use of certain drugs, such as alcohol, mescalin, and lysergic acid. Whereas alcohol dulls the clarity of awareness, mescalin and lysergic acid do not. Consequently these two, and sometimes also nitrous oxide and carbon dioxide, will induce states of consciousness in which the individual feels his relational identity with the whole realm of nature. Although these states appear to be similar to those realized through more "natural" means, they differ in the sense that being able to swim with a life jacket differs from swimming unaided. From personal, though limited, experimentation with a research group working with lysergic acid, I would judge that the state of consciousness induced is confused with a mystical state because of similarities of language used in describing the two. The experience is multidimensional, as if everything were inside, or implied, everything else, requiring a description which is paradoxical from the standpoint of ordinary logic. But whereas the drug gives a vision of nature which is infinitely complex, the mystical state is clarifying, and gives a vision which is as infinitely simple. The drug seems to give the intelligence a kaleidescopic quality which "patterns" the perception of relations in accordance with its own peculiar structure.

the child tries to speed up his neural skills by sheer muscle-power.

For all that has been said, we are so convinced of the necessity of mental strain that the dropping of the habit will hardly be acceptable until certain theoretical objections are answered. The "mental strain" deplored by conventional psychology is, of course, highly excessive strain, but it is not generally recognized that there is a contradiction in mental strain as such and in any degree. The two principal objections are, I think, firstly, that an absence of strain would encourage a view of the world characterized by mystical and pantheistic vagueness which is both demoralizing and uncritical; and, secondly, that since mental strain is essential to any self-control, its absence will result in being completely swept away by one's feelings.

In theological circles "pantheism" has long been a definitively damning label, and those who like their religious and philosophical opinions to be robust and definite are also inclined to use the word "mysticism" with the same kind of opprobrium. They associate it with "mist," with vagueness, with clouding of issues and blurring of distinctions. Therefore from this standpoint nothing could be more ghastly than "mystical pantheism" or "pantheistic nature mysticism," which is just what the attitude of *kuan* appears to produce. However much the contrary may be pointed out, such people continue to insist that Taoist and Buddhist mysticism reduces the interesting and significant distinctions of the world to a miasma of uniform oneness.[12]

[12] In my *Supreme Identity* I put forward a view of the Vedanta which very carefully explained its difference from pantheism and from all those types of "acosmistic" mysticsm which seem to idealize the complete disappearance of the natural world from consciousness. Nevertheless, it was criticized by Reinhold Niebuhr in *The Nation* for advocating exactly those views which it opposed, an interesting example of the fact that Christian polemicists spend a good deal of energy attacking points of view which exist only in their own minds.

I am God, you are God, everything is God, and God is a boundless and featureless sea of dimly conscious tapioca pudding. The mystic is thus a feeble-minded fellow who finds in this boring "undifferentiated aesthetic continuum" (Northrop) a source of enthusiasm, because, somehow or other, it unifies the conflicts and evils of the world into a transcendental Goodness.

While this is obviously an ignorant caricature, there is something to be said in defense of philosophical vagueness. Strangely assorted people join forces in making fun of it—Logical Positivists and Catholic Neo-Thomists, Dialectical Materialists and Protestant Neo-Orthodoxists, Behaviorists and Fundamentalists. Despite intense differences of opinion among themselves, they belong to a psychological type which takes special glee in having one's philosophy of life clear-cut, hard, and rigid. They range from the kind of scientist who likes to lick his tongue around the notion of "brute" facts to the kind of religionist who fondles a system of "unequivocal dogma." There is doubtless a deep sense of security in being able to say, "The clear and authoritative teaching of the Church is . . . ," or to feel that one has mastered a logical method which can tear other opinions, and especially metaphysical opinions, to shreds. Attitudes of this kind usually go together with a somewhat aggressive and hostile type of personality which employs sharp definition like the edge of a sword. There is more in this than a metaphor, for, as we have seen, the laws and hypotheses of science are not so much discoveries as instruments, like knives and hammers, for bending nature to one's will. So there is a type of personality which approaches the world with an entire armory of sharp and hard instruments, by means of which it slices and sorts the universe into precise and sterile categories which will not interfere with one's peace of mind.

There is a place in life for a sharp knife, but there is a still more important place for other kinds of contact with the world. Man is not to be an intellectual porcupine, meeting his environment with a surface of spikes. Man meets the world outside with a soft skin, with a delicate eyeball and eardrum, and finds communion with it through a warm, melting, vaguely defined, and caressing touch whereby the world is not set at a distance like an enemy to be shot, but embraced to become one flesh, like a beloved wife. After all, the whole possibility of clear knowledge depends upon sensitive organs which, as it were, bring the outside world into our bodies, and give us knowledge of that world precisely in the form of our own bodily states.

Hence the importance of opinions, of instruments of the mind, which are vague, misty, and melting rather than clear-cut. They provide possibilties of communication, of actual contact and relationship with nature more intimate than anything to be found by preserving at all costs the "distance of objectivity." As Chinese and Japanese painters have so well understood, there are landscapes which are best viewed through half-closed eyes, mountains which are most alluring when partially veiled in mist, and waters which are most profound when the horizon is lost, and they are merged with the sky.

> Through the evening mist a lone goose is flying;
> Of one tone are wide waters and sky.

Or consider Po Chü-i's lines on "Walking at Night in Fine Rain," translated, I think, by Arthur Walcy:

> Autumn clouds, vague and obscure;
> The evening, lonely and chill.
> I felt the dampness on my garments,
> But saw no spot, and heard no sound of rain.

Or Lin Yutang's version of Chia Tao's "Searching for the Hermit in Vain":

> *I asked the boy beneath the pines.*
> *He said, "The Master's gone alone*
> *Herb-picking somewhere on the mount,*
> *Cloud-hidden, whereabouts unknown."*

Images of a rather similar mood are strung together by Seami when he tries to suggest what the Japanese mean by *yugen*, a subtle order of beauty whose origin is dark and obscure: "To watch the sun sink behind a flower-clad hill, to wander on and on in a huge forest with no thought of return, to stand on the shore and gaze after a boat that goes hid by far-off islands, to ponder on the journey of wild geese seen and lost among the clouds." [13] But there is a kind of brash mental healthiness ever ready to rush in and clean up the mystery, to find out just precisely where the wild geese have gone, what herbs the master is picking and where, and that sees the true face of a landscape only in the harsh light of the noonday sun. It is just this attitude which every traditional culture finds utterly insufferable in Western man, not just because it is tactless and unrefined, but because it is blind. It cannot tell the difference between the surface and the depth. It seeks the depth by cutting into the surface. But the depth is known only when it reveals itself, and ever withdraws from the probing mind. In the words of Chuang-tzu:

> Things are produced around us, but no one knows the whence. They issue forth, but no one sees the portal. Men one and all value that part of knowledge which is known. They do not know how to avail themselves of the unknown in order to reach knowledge. Is not this misguided? [14]

[13] Waley (1), pp. 21–22.
[14] H. A. Giles (1), p. 345.

We fail so easily to see the difference between fear of the unknown and respect for the unknown, thinking that those who do not hasten in with bright lights and knives are deterred by a holy and superstitious fear. Respect for the unknown is the attitude of those who, instead of raping nature, woo her until she gives herself. But what she gives, even then, is not the cold clarity of the surface but the warm inwardness of the body—a mysteriousness which is not merely a negation, a blank absence of knowledge, but that positive substance which we call wonderfull.

> "The highest that man can attain in these matters," said Goethe, "is wonder; if the primary phenomenon causes this, let him be satisfied; more it cannot bring; and he should forbear to seek for anything further behind it: here is the limit. But the sight of a prime phenomenon is generally not enough for people. They think they must go still further; and are thus like children, who, after peeping into a mirror, turn it round directly to see what is on the other side." [15]

For as Whitehead said:

> When you understand all about the sun and all about the atmosphere and all about the rotation of the earth, you may still miss the radiance of the sunset. There is no substitute for the direct perception [kuan] of the concrete achievement of a thing in its actuality. [16]

This is, surely, a true materialism, or perhaps it would be better to say a true substantialism, since matter is really cognate to "meter" and properly designates not the reality of nature but nature in terms of measures. And "substance" in this sense would not be the gross notion of "stuff," but what is conveyed by the Chinese *t'i* [17]—the wholeness, the

[15] Eckermann (1). February 18th, 1829.
[16] Whitehead (1), p. 248.
[17] M 6246.

Gestalt, the complete field of relations, which escapes every linear description.

The natural world therefore reveals its content, its fullness of wonder, when respect hinders us from investigating it in such a way as to shatter it to abstractions. If I *must* cross every skyline to find out what is beyond, I shall never appreciate the true depth of sky seen between trees upon the ridge of a hill. If I must map the canyons and count the trees, I shall never enter into the sound of a hidden waterfall. If I must explore and investigate every trail, that path which vanishes into the forest far up on the mountainside will be found at last to lead merely back to the suburbs. To the mind which pursues every road to its end, every road leads nowhere. To abstain is not to postpone the cold disillusionment of the true facts but to see that one arrives by staying rather than going, that to be forever looking beyond is to remain blind to what is here.

To know nature, the Tao, and the "substance" of things, we must know it as, in the archaic sense, a man "knows" a woman—in the warm vagueness of immediate contact. As the *Cloud of Unknowing* says of God, "By love he may be gotten and holden, but by thought never." This implies, too, that it is also mistaken to think of it as *actually* vague, like mist or diffused light or tapioca pudding. The image of vagueness implies that to know nature, outside ourselves as within, we must abandon every idea, every thought and opinion, of what it is—and look. If we must have some idea of it, it must be the most vague imaginable, which is why, even for Westerners, such formless conceptions as the Tao are to be preferred to the idea of God, with its all too definite associations.

The danger of the "pantheistic" and mystical attitude to nature is, of course, that it may become exclusive and one-sided, though there seem to be few historical instances of this. There is no real reason why it should become so, for its advantage is precisely that it gives us a formless background against which the forms of everyday, practical problems may be seen more clearly. When our idea of the background, of God, is highly formal, practical conduct is as tortuous as trying to write upon a printed page. Issues cannot be seen clearly because it is not seen that matters of right and wrong are like the rules of grammar—conventions of communication. By grounding right and wrong in the Absolute, in the background, not only do the rules become too rigid, but they are also sanctioned by too weighty an authority. As a Chinese proverb says, "Do not swat a fly upon your friend's head with a hatchet." By grounding the rules of action in God, the West has not succeeded in fostering any unusual degree of morality. On the contrary, it has invited just those violent ideological revolutions against intolerable authority which are so characteristic of its history. The same would apply to a rigid scientific dogma as to what is natural and what is not.

In practice a mysticism which avoids all rigid formulations of both nature and God has usually been favorable to the growth of science.[18] For its attitude is empirical, emphasizing concrete experience rather than theoretical construction or belief, and its frame of mind is contemplative and receptive. It is unfavorable to science to the degree that science confuses abstract models with nature, and to the degree that science, as technology, interferes with nature myopically, or upon the basis of prescientific views of man from which it has not recovered. Furthermore, it provides a basis for action which is not a cumbersome linear and legal view either of God's will or of laws of nature based on an accumulation of *past* experiment.

[18] On which see Needham (1), vol. 2, pp. 89–98.

The attitude of *kuan* is peculiarly sensitive to the conditions of the immediate moment in all their changeful interrelatedness, and, as we have seen, one of the difficulties of scientific knowledge is that its linear complexity makes it hard to apply to swift decisions, especially when "circumstances alter cases." Thus in discussing the secrets of successful drama Seami wrote:

> If you look deeply into the ultimate essentials of this art, you will find that what is called "the flower" [of *yugen*] has no separate existence. Were it not for the spectator who reads into the performance a thousand excellences, there would be no "flower" at all. The Sutra says, "Good and ill are one; villainy and honesty are of like kind." Indeed, what standard have we whereby to discern good from bad? We can only take what suits the need of the moment and call it "good." [19]

Such an attitude would be short-sighted indeed if it were based on the linear and punctive view of the moment, where each "thing" is not seen in its relation to the whole.[20] For example, those whom we hate most violently are often those we love most deeply, and if we are insensitive to this interrelation we may confuse the part feeling with the whole, and destroy someone we love or marry someone we are going to hate.

[19] Waley (1), p. 22.

[20] An excellent example of sensitivity to the moment is found in the application of Zen to *kendo*, or swordsmanship. No amount of drilled-in rules or reflexes can prepare the swordsman for the infinity of different attacks which he may have to face, especially when confronted with more than one opponent. He is taught, therefore, never to make any specific preparation for attack nor to expect it from any particular direction. Otherwise, to meet an unusual attack he will have to retreat from one stance before being able to adopt another. He must be able to spring immediately from a relaxed center of rest to the direction required. This relaxed openness of sensitivity in every direction is precisely *kuan*, or, as it is more commonly called in Zen, *mushin*, which is to say no "mind," no strain of the mind to watch for a particular result.

This brings us, then, to the second theoretical objection: that the mental strain of the controlling ego is necessary if we are not to be carried away by naturally undisciplined feelings and emotions. The objection is, once again, based on a political instead of an organic view of human nature. Human psychology is seen as composed of separate parts, functions, or faculties, as if the Lord God had made him by grafting the soul of an angel to the body of an animal. Man is then conceived as a collection of powers, urges, and appetites to be governed by the ego-soul. It is obvious at once that this view has had a profound influence upon modern psychology, which, though advising the ego to govern with kindness rather than violence, still treats it as the responsible boss.

But if we think of the total course of a man's experience, inner and outer, together with its unconscious psychophysical bases, as a system regulated organically, the principle of control must be entirely different.

Joy and anger, sorrow and happiness, caution and remorse, come upon us by turns, with ever-changing mood. They come like music from hollows (in wood, when played upon by the wind), or like mushrooms from the damp. Daily and nightly they alternate within us, but we cannot tell whence they spring. . . .

But for these emotions I should not be. But for me, they would have no scope. So far we can go; but we do not know what it is that brings them into play. If there is really a governor [*tsai*, M 6655], we find no evidence of its being. One could believe that it might be active, but we do not see its form. It would have to have feeling without form.

The hundred bones, the nine orifices, and the six internal organs are all complete in their places. Which of them should one prefer? Do we like them all equally, or some more than others? Are they all the servants [of another]?

Are these servants unable to govern one another mutually, or do they take the parts of ruler and servant alternately? [21]

Taking up this theme in his commentary on Chuang-tzu, Kuo Hsiang says:

> The hands and feet differ in their duties; the five internal organs differ in their functions. They never associate with one another, yet the hundred parts (of the body) are held together by them in a common unity. This is the way in which they associate through non-association. They never (deliberately) cooperate, and yet, both internally and externally, all complete one another. This is the way in which they cooperate through non-cooperation. [22]

In other words, all parts of the organism regulate themselves spontaneously (*tzu-jan*), and their order is confused when the changing panorama of feelings seems to be confronted by a controlling ego, which attempts to retain the positive (*yang*) and to reject the negative (*yin*).

According to Taoist philosophy, it is just this attempt to regulate the psyche from outside and to wrest the positive from the negative which is at the root of all social and moral confusion. What needs, then, to be controlled is not so much the spontaneous flow of human passions as the ego which exploits them—in other words, the controller itself. This has likewise been evident to such highly perceptive Christians as St. Augustine and Martin Luther, who realized so keenly that mere *self*-control was in no sense a remedy for the ills of man since it was precisely in the self that evil had taken its root. But they never abandoned the political idea of control, since their solution was to have the self empowered and regenerated by the grace of God—the ego of the universe. They did not see that the difficulty lay, not in the good or ill will of the controller,

---

[21] *Chuang-tzu, ii.* Cf. H. A. Giles (1), p. 14, Lin Yutang (2), p. 235, and Needham (1), vol. 2, p. 52.

[22] *Chuang-tzu Chu, iii,* 25. Tr. Bodde in Fung Yu-lan (1), vol. 2, p. 211.

but in the whole rationale of control which they were attempting to use. They did not realize that the problem
for God was the same as the problem for the human ego.
For even God's universe had spawned the Devil, who
arises not so much from his own independent malice as
from God's "arrogance" in assuming omnipotent kingship
and identifying himself with unalloyed goodness. The
Devil is God's unconsciously produced shadow. Naturally,
God is not allowed to be responsible for the origin of evil,
for the connection between the two lies in the unconscious.
Man says, "I didn't mean to hurt you, but my temper got
the better of me. I shall try to control it in future." And
God says, "I didn't mean there to be any evil, but my angel
Lucifer brought it up of his own free will. In the future I
will shut him up safely in hell." [23]

A problem of evil arises as soon as there is a problem of
good, that is, as soon as there is any thought of what may
be done to make the present situation "better," under
whatever nomenclature the idea may be concealed. Taoist
philosophy may easily be misunderstood as saying that it
is better to let an organic system regulate itself than to
meddle in it from without, and better to recognize that
good and evil are correlative than to wrest the one from
the other. And yet Chuang-tzu says plainly:

> Those who would have right without its correlative,
> wrong; or good government without its correlative, misrule,
> —they do not apprehend the great principles of the universe
> nor the conditions to which all creation is subject. One
> might as well talk of the existence of heaven without that
> of earth, or of the negative principle without the positive,
> which is clearly absurd. Such people, if they do not yield to
> argument, must be either fools or knaves.[24] *xvii*

[23] For a fuller discussion of this theme see Jung (1), and Watts (2), ch.
2.
[24] H. A. Giles (1), pp. 207–8.

Yet, if this be true, must there not be fools and knaves as the correlatives of sages and saints, and does not the fallacy attacked simply reappear in the attack?

If the positive and the negative, the good and the evil, are indeed correlative, no course of action can be recommended, including even the course of inaction. Nothing will make anything better which will not also make it worse. But this is exactly the predicament of the human ego as Taoist philosophy sees it. It is always wanting to control its situation so as to improve it, but neither action nor, with the motive of improvement, inaction will succeed. Recognizing the trap in which it finds itself, the mind has no alternative but to surrender that "straining after the good" which constitutes the ego. It does not surrender cunningly, with the thought that this will make things better. It surrenders unconditionally—not because it is good to do nothing, but because nothing can be done. All at once there descends upon it, quite spontaneously, a profound and completely uncontrived stillness—a quietude that envelops the world like the first fall of heavy snow, or like a windless afternoon in the mountains, where silence makes itself known in the undisturbed hum of insects in the grass.

In this stillness there is no sense of passivity, of submitting to necessity, for there is no longer any differentiation between the mind and its experience. All acts, one's own and others', seem to be happening freely from a single source. Life keeps moving on, and yet remains profoundly rooted in the present, seeking no result, for the present has spread out from its constriction in an elusive pin-point of strained consciousness to an all-embracing eternity. Feelings both positive and negative come and go without turmoil, for they seem to be simply observed, though there is no one observing. They pass trackless like birds in the sky, and build up no resistances which have to be dissipated in reckless action.

Clearly this state is, in retrospect, "better" than the seeking and staring strain of the mind which came before. But its goodness is of another order. Because it came unsought, it is not the kind of goodness which is in relation to evil, not the fantasy of peace which is conceived in the midst of turmoil. Furthermore, since nothing is done to retain it, it is not in relation to the memory of the former state, which otherwise would move one to fortify and protect it against change. For now there is no one left to build the fortifications. Memories rise and fall like other feelings, ordered perhaps better than before, but no longer congealing around an ego to build its illusion of continued identity.

From this standpoint it can be seen that intelligence is not a separate, ordering faculty of the mind, but a characteristic of the whole organism-environment relationship, the field of forces wherein lies the reality of a human being. For as Macneile Dixon said in his *Human Situation*, "Tangible and visible things are but the poles, or terminations of these fields of unperceived energy. Matter, if it exists at all in any sense, is a sleeping partner in the firm of Nature." Between subject and object, organism and environment, *yang* and *yin*, is the balancing or homeostatic relationship called Tao—intelligent not because it has an ego but because it has *li*, organic pattern. The spontaneous flow of feeling, rising and falling in its mood, is an essential part of this balancing process, and is not, then, to be regarded as the disordered play of blind passions. Thus it is said that Lieh-tzu attained the Tao by "letting the events of the heart go just as they liked." [25] As a good sailor gives

---

[25] *Lieh-tzu*, 2. L. Giles (1), p. 41, translates this passage, "my mind (*hsin*) gave free rein to its reflections (*nien*)," but this is rather too

himself to the motion of a ship and does not fight it with his stomach muscles, the man of Tao gives himself to the motion of his moods.

Surprisingly, perhaps, this is not at all the same thing as is ordinarily meant by "giving in to one's feelings"—always a symptom of resistance rather than "give." For when we think about our feelings we tend to represent them as fixed states. Such words as anger, depression, fear, grief, anxiety, and guilt suggest uniform states which tend to persist if no action is taken to change or release them. As fever was once considered a disease instead of a natural healing process, we still think of negative feelings as disorders of the mind which need to be cured. But what needs to be cured is the inner resistance to those feelings which moves us to dissipate them in precipitate action. To resist the feeling is to be unable to contain it long enough for it to work itself out. Anger, for example, is not a fixed state but a motion, and unless compressed by resistance into unusual violence, like boiling water in a sealed vessel, it will adjust itself spontaneously. For anger is not a separate, autonomous demon rushing up from time to time from his quarters in the unconscious. Anger is simply a direction or pattern of psychic action. There is thus no anger; there is only acting angrily, or feeling angrily. Anger is feeling in motion to some other "state," for as Lao-tzu said:

> A swishing wind does not outlast the morning; pelting rain does not outlast the day. Who makes these things but heaven and earth? If heaven and earth cannot maintain them for long, how can man? *xxiii*

intellectual since *hsin* (M 2735) is not so much the thinking mind as the totality of psychic functioning, conscious and unconscious, and *nien* (M 4716) is not so much cortical thought as any event of psychic experience.

To give free rein to the course of feeling is therefore to observe it without interference, recognizing that because feeling is motion it is not to be understood in terms which imply not only static states but judgments of good and bad. Watched without naming, feelings become simply neuromuscular tensions and changes, palpitations and pressures, tinglings and twitchings, of enormous subtlety and interest. This is, however, not quite the same thing as the psychotherapeutic gambit of "accepting" negative feelings *in order* to change them, that is, with the intention of effecting a shift of the whole tone of feeling in the direction of the positive and "good." "Acceptance" of this kind still implies the ego, standing apart from the immediate feeling or experience, and waiting for it to change—however patiently and submissively.

So long as the sense of the observing subject remains, there is the effort, however indirect, to control feeling from the outside, which is resistance setting up turmoil in the stream. Resistance disappears and the balancing process comes into full effect not by intention on the part of the subject, but only as it is seen that the feeling of being the subject, the ego, is itself part of the stream of experience and does not stand outside it in a controlling position. In the words of Chuang-tzu:

> Only the truly intelligent understand this principle of the identity of all things. They do not view things as apprehended by themselves, subjectively, but transfer themselves into the position of the things viewed. And viewing them thus they are able to comprehend them, nay, to master them.[26]

However, the point might be expressed more exactly by saying that the subject is treated not as an object but as the inseparable pole or term of a subject-object identity.

[26] *Chuang-tzu*, 2. Tr. H. A. Giles (1), p. 20.

The dividedness of the knower and the known becomes, without being simply obliterated, the plainest sign of their inner unity.

This is, indeed, the crucial point of the whole unitive philosophy of nature as it is set forward in Taoism and Buddhism, and which distinguishes it from a merely monistic pantheism. Distinct and unique events, whether external objects or the internal subject, are seen to be "one with nature" by virtue of their very distinctness, and not at all by absorption into a featureless uniformity. Once again, it is the mutual distinction of figure and ground, subject and object, and not their merging which reveals their inner identity. A Zen master was asked, "I have heard that there is one thing which cannot be named. It has not been born; it will not die when the body dies. When the universe burns up it will not be affected. What is that one thing?" The master answered, "A sesame bun."

In addition, then, to the mood of *yugen*, of mysterious and pregnant vagueness, which haunts Far Eastern painting, there is also an immensely forceful delineation of the unique event—the single bird, the spray of bamboo, the solitary tree, the lonely rock. Hence the sudden awakening to this "inner identity" which in Zen is called *satori* is usually precipitated by, or bound up with, some such simple fact as the sound of a berry falling in the forest or the sight of a piece of crumpled paper in the street. There is thus a double meaning in Suzuki's translation of the poem:

> *Oh, this one rare occurrence,*
> *For which would I not be glad to give ten thou-*
> *   sand pieces of gold!*
> *A hat is on my head, a bundle round my loins;*
> *And on my staff the refreshing breeze and the*
> *   full moon I carry!*

For the "one rare occurrence" is at once the *satori* experience and the unique event to which it is attached—one
implying all, moment implying eternity. But to *state* the
implication is, in a way, to say too much, especially if it
were taken to mean that the perception of the particular
ought to make us think about the universal. On the contrary, the universality of the unique event and the eternity
of the moment come to be seen only as the straining of
the mind is released and the present event, whatever it
may be, is regarded without the slightest attempt to get
anything from it. However, this attempt is so habitual that
it can hardly be stopped, so that whenever anyone tries
to accept the moment just as it is he becomes aware only
of the frustration of himself trying to do so. This seems to
present an unbreakable vicious circle—unless he realizes
that the moment which he was trying to accept has now
moved on and is presenting itself to him as his own sensation of strain! If he feels it to be voluntary, there is no
problem in accepting it, for it is his own immediate act. If
he feels it to be involuntary, he must perforce accept it,
for he can do no other. Either way, the strain is accepted
and it dissolves. But this is also the discovery of the inner
identity of the voluntary and the involuntary, the subjective and the objective. For when the object, the moment to be accepted, presented itself as the sensation of
the strain of trying to accept, this was the subject, the
ego itself. In the words of the Zen master P'u-yen, "Nothing is left to you at this moment but to burst out into a
loud laugh. You have accomplished a final turning and in
very truth know that 'when a cow in Kuai-chou grazes
the herbage, a horse in I-chou finds its stomach filled.' " [27]

In sum, then, the realization that nature is ordered
organically rather than politically, that it is a field of relationships rather than a collection of things, requires an

[27] Suzuki (3), p. 80.

appropriate mode of human awareness. The habitual egocentric mode in which man identifies himself with a subject facing a world of alien objects does not fit the physical
situation. So long as it remains, our inward feeling is at
variance with reality. Based on this feeling, our efforts to
control ourselves and the surrounding world become vi-
ciously circular entanglements of ever-growing complexity.
More and more the individual feels himself frustrated and
impotent in the midst of a mechanical world order which
has become an irresistible "march of progress" toward
ends of its own. Therapies for the frustrated individual,
whether religious or psychological, merely complicate the
problem in so far as they assume that the separate ego is
the very reality toward which their ministrations are directed. For, as Trigant Burrow saw, the source of the
trouble is social rather than individual: that is to say, the
ego is a social convention foisted upon human consciousness by conditioning. The root of mental disorder is not
therefore a malfunctioning peculiar to this or that ego; it
is rather that the ego-feeling as such is an error of perception. To placate it is only to enable it to go on confusing
the mind with a mode of awareness which, because it
clashes with the natural order, breeds the vast family of
psychological frustrations and illnesses.

An organic natural order has its proper correspondence
in a mode of consciousness which is a total feeling or
experiencing. Where feeling is broken up into the feeler
and the feeling, the knower and the known, what lies between the two is not relationship but mere juxtaposition.
Identified with one of its terms alone, consciousness feels
"out on a limb" facing an alien world which it controls
only to find it more and more uncontrollable, and which it
exploits only to find it more and more ungratifying.

4: The World as Ecstasy

DEEPLY INVOLVED WITH OUR WHOLE ES-
trangement from nature is the embarrassment of "having" a body. It is perhaps an egg-and-hen question as to
whether we resent the body because we think we are
spirits, or *vice versa*. But we are accustomed to feeling
that our bodies are vehicles in which we are compelled
to live, vehicles which are at once all too much ourselves
and yet utterly foreign. Responding only most imperfectly
to the will and resisting the comprehension of the intellect, the body seems to be thrust upon us like an indispensable wife with whom it is impossible to live. We love
it most dearly, and yet must spend most of our time working to support it. Its five senses, delicate and vibrant, communicate the whole delight and glory of the world at the
price of being equally receptive to its agony and horror.
For the body is sensitive because it is soft, pliant, and im-
pressionable, but it lives in a universe which is for the
most part rock and fire. When young we let our consciousness expand with joy through all the innumerable passages
of its nerves, but as time goes on we begin to withdraw,
and beg the surgeon to "fix" it like a wayward machine,
to cut away the pieces which rot and ache, and to dope the
jangling senses which so inconsiderately retain their alert-
ness while all else deteriorates. Modestly and graciously
posed, the naked form of man or woman is revered as the
height of beauty, yet this same form can turn in an instant
lascivious or grotesque, disgusting or uncouth, by the slight-

est change of posture or activity—so easily, indeed, that for most of the time we conceal it from sight with clothing, beneath which it grows pallid and potatoish like the white slugs that live under rocks.

The body is so alien to the mind that even when it is at its best it is not so much loved as exploited, and for the remainder of the time we do what we may to put it in a state of comfort where it may be forgotten, where its limitations will not encumber the play of emotion and thought. But contrive as we will to transcend this physical vehicle, the clarity of consciousness goes hand in hand with the sensitivity of nerves and thus with inevitable exposure to revulsion and pain. This is so much so that the hardness and painfulness of things become the measure of their reality. What does not resist us becomes dreamlike and impalpable, but in the shock of pain we *know* that we are alive and awake, and thus come to think of the real as that which conflicts most abruptly with the whole nature of sensitivity. One has thus never heard of soft facts, only of hard. Yet it is just because there are such soft facts as eyeballs and finger-tips that the hard are manifested.

But to the extent that the measure of reality is felt to be the degree of resistance and pain which the environment offers to our nerves, the body becomes above all else the instrument of our suffering. It negates our will; it decays before we have lost the capacity for disgust; its possession exposes us to all the twenty-one measurable degrees of agony by the cruelty of human torture, by accident, or by disease. Those who are fortunate enough to escape the worst that can happen are nevertheless tormented with imaginations of what might be, and their skins tingle and their stomachs turn in sympathy and horror at the fate of others.

It is little wonder, then, that we seek detachment from

the body, wanting to convince ourselves that the real "I" is not this quaking mass of tissue with all its repulsive possibilities for pain and corruption. It is little wonder that we expect religions, philosophies, and other forms of wisdom to show us above all else a way of deliverance from suffering, from the plight of being a soft body in a world of hard reality. Sometimes therefore it seems that the answer is to match hardness with hardness, to identify ourselves with a spirit which has principles but no feelings, to despise and mortify the body, and to withdraw into the comfortably fleshless world of abstract thought or psychic fantasy. To match the hardness of facts we then identify our minds with such symbols of fixity, entity, and power as the ego, the will, and the immortal soul, believing ourselves to belong in our inmost being to a realm of spirit beyond both the hardness of fact and the weakness of flesh. This is, as it were, a shrinking of consciousness from its environment of pain, gathering itself back and back into a knot around its own center.

Yet it is just in this shrinking and hardening that consciousness not only loses its true strength but also aggravates its plight. For the withdrawal from suffering is also suffering, such that the restricted and enclosed consciousness of the ego is really a spasm of fear. As a man with a stomach wound craves water, which it is fatal to drink, the mind's chronic withdrawal from suffering renders it just that much more vulnerable. Fully expanded, consciousness feels an identity with the whole world, but contracted it is the more inescapably attached to a single minute and perishable organism.

This is not to say that it is fatal for nerves and muscles to draw back from a sharp spike or some other occasion of pain, for did they not do so the organism would swiftly cease to exist. The withdrawal I am speaking of here is much deeper: it is a withdrawal from withdrawal, an unwillingness to be capable of feeling pain, unwillingness to squirm and shrink when the occasion of pain arises. Subtle as this distinction may be, it is of immense importance, though it may seem at first that pain and the unwillingness to react painfully are the same thing. But it must be obvious that unless the organism can feel pain, it cannot withdraw from danger, so that the unwillingness to be able to be hurt is in fact suicidal, whereas the simple retreat from an occasion of pain is not. It is true that we want to have our cake and eat it: we want to be sensitive and alive, but not sensitive to suffering. But this puts us in a contradiction of the specially intolerable type known as a "double bind."

The "double bind" is a situation wherein all the alternatives offered are forbidden. A witness in court is put in a double bind when the attorney asks him, "Have you stopped beating your wife? Answer yes or no!" Either answer will convict him of beating her. So also when suffering arises we want to escape both from its objective occasion and from its subjective reactions. But when escape from the former is impossible, so is escape from the latter. We *must* suffer—that is, we must react in the only way that is open to us, which would naturally be to writhe, shriek, or weep. Now the double bind comes in when we forbid ourselves this reaction, either in actual suffering or in the imagination of suffering to come. We revolt at the prospect of our own orgiastic reactions to pain because they are in flat contradiction with our socially conditioned image of ourselves. Such reactions are a fearful admission of the identity of consciousness with the organism, of the lack of a detached, powerful, and transcending will which is the essential core of the personality.

Hence the sadist and torturer takes his most unholy delight not just in watching the bodily convulsions of his victim, but in "breaking the spirit" which resists them. Yet if there were no resisting spirit his savagery would be rendered something like slashing at water with a sword, and he would find himself confronted with a total weakness that offered neither challenge nor interest. But it is exactly this weakness which is the mind's real and unsuspected strength. In Lao-tzu's words:

> Man when living is soft and tender; when dead he is hard and tough. All animals and plants are tender and fragile; when dead they become withered and dry. Therefore it is said: the hard and the tough are parts of death; the soft and tender are parts of life. This is the reason why the soldiers when they are too tough cannot carry the day; the tree when it is too tough will break. The position of the strong and great is low, and the position of the weak and tender is high.[1] *lxxvi*

There appear, then, to be two unexpected consequences of unreservedly permitting the organism its natural, orgiastic response to pain, of which one is the ability to endure pain and its anticipation by reason of a far greater amount of "give" in the system. The other is that this, in turn, cuts down the total shock of suffering upon the organism, which furthermore reduces the intensity of the reactions. In other words, the toughening of the spirit against suffering and the shrinking of consciousness from the orgiastic reactions which it involves are a socially inculcated error of behavior, making the human situation far worse than it need be. Moreover, this shrinking of consciousness from our reactions to suffering is at root the same psychological mechanism as the straining of consciousness to get the most from our reactions to pleasure,

[1] In Ch'u Ta-kao (1), p. 89.

and both make up the sensation of the separate, indwelling ego.

This is surely the reason why so many spiritual traditions insist that the way to liberation from egocentricity is through suffering. Yet this is so often misunderstood as "practice suffering," as toughening oneself against suffering by increasing doses of mortification to harden the body and soul. Interpreted in this way, the spiritual discipline of suffering becomes a way of death and insensitivity, of final withdrawal from life into a "spiritual" world which is totally removed from nature. It is to correct this error that Mahayana Buddhism maintains that "nirvana and samsara are not different," that the state of liberation is not away from the state of nature, and that the liberated Bodhisattva returns indefinitely into the "round of birth-and-death" out of his compassion for all sentient beings. For the same reason Buddhist doctrine denies the reality of a separate ego, saying:

> Suffering alone exists, none who suffer;
> The deed there is, but no doer thereof;
> Nirvana is, but no one seeking it;
> Path there is, but none who travel it.[2]

And again, unexpectedly, the dissolution of the egocentric contraction (*sankocha*) of consciousness by no means reduces the personality to a flabby nonentity. On the contrary, the organism is at its greatest strength in realizing the fullest possible relation to its environment—a relation which is hardly felt at all when the individualized consciousness tries to preserve itself by separation from the body and from all that it experiences. "Whosoever would save his soul shall lose it," and we should understand this "save" as "salvage," as enclosing and isolating. Conversely,

[2] *Visuddhimagga*, 16.

we should understand that the soul or personality lives just to the degree that it does not withdraw, that it does not shrink from the full implications of being one with the body and with the whole realm of natural experience. For although this seems to suggest the absorption of man into the flux of nature, the integrity of personality is far better preserved by the faith of self-giving than the shattering anxiety of self-preservation.

We saw that the shrinking of consciousness from suffering and the straining of consciousness to seek gratification are at root the same. In each case the way of dissolution is also the same, and involves first of all the recognition that consciousness, in so far as it feels itself to be the ego, cannot stop its own shrinking, its revulsion from the orgiastic response to pain. It must therefore be understood that this revulsion is itself part and parcel of the orgiastic response, and not, as we are led to believe, a means of escape from it. This is, in other words, the recognition that all our psychological defenses against suffering are useless. The more we defend, the more we suffer, and defending is itself suffering. Although we cannot help putting up the psychological defense, it dissolves when it is seen that the defense is all of a piece with what we are defending ourselves against. The entire movement is the convulsion *of* suffering which does not lead *away* from suffering. Continued as a means to get rid of suffering, it merely intensifies it. But continued because this is simply the natural response to which, if we do not deceive ourselves, we *must* give in, the whole experience of suffering undergoes a startling change.

It becomes what in Indian philosophy is called *ananda,* ordinarily translated "bliss." *Ananda* is attributed to Brahman, the ultimate Reality beyond all dualities, together with *sat,* truth, and *chit,* awareness. Yet we usually consider bliss to be an extremely dualistic state of mind—an extreme of happiness or pleasure, opposed to an equal extreme of misery or pain. There would seem to be a serious contradiction in making anything so relative as bliss one of the attributes of the Absolute. For if bliss is realized in contrast with abject misery as light is known in contrast with darkness, how is it possible to contemplate a bliss which is nondual and eternal?

It must first be understood that Indian philosophy uses a convention of terminology similar to the trick of perspective, of representing a three-dimensional object upon a two-dimensional surface. Any line drawn upon a flat surface will be more or less horizontal or perpendicular, spanning the height and the width of the area. But by the convention of perspective, slanting lines which approach a vanishing point are understood to represent the third dimension of depth. As the flat surface has but two dimensions, so our ordinary thought and language has a rigidly dualistic logic, in terms of which it makes no sense to speak of that which "neither is nor is not," nor of a bliss which transcends both pleasure and pain. But just as one can suggest three dimensions in terms of two, dualistic language can suggest an experience beyond duality. The very word "nondual" (*advaita*) is, formally speaking, the opposite of "dual" (*dvaita*), as bliss is the opposite of misery. But Indian philosophy uses *advaita* and *ananda* in a context where they refer to another dimension of experience, as lines that are more or less high or wide are taken to signify depth. Furthermore, this other dimension of experience is understood to be of a higher order of reality than the dualistic dimension, where life and death, pleasure and pain stand utterly apart.

What we feel is to an enormous and unsuspected degree dependent on what we think, and the basic contrasts of

thought ordinarily strike us as the basic contrasts of the
natural world. We therefore take it for granted that we *feel*
an immense difference between pleasure and pain. But
it is obvious in some of the milder forms of these sensations
that the pleasure or the pain lies not so much in the feeling
itself as in its context. There is no appreciable physiological difference between shudders of delight and shudders of
fear, nor between the thrills of rapturous music and the
thrills of terrifying melodrama. Likewise, intensities of joy
and grief produce the same "heartbreak" feeling which is
expressed in weeping, and to fall deeply in love is to enter
a state where delight and anguish are at times so inter-
woven as to be indistinguishable. But the context of the
feeling changes its interpretation, depending on whether
the circumstances which arouse it are for us or against
us. Similarly, one and the same verbal sound changes its
meaning according to the setting, as in Thomas Hood's

> They went and told the sexton,
> And the sexton tolled the bell.

It is easy enough to see the sensational or physiological
identity of these feelings in some of the milder forms of
physical pleasure and pain, and even in some of the strong
forms of moral pleasure and pain. But it is exceedingly
difficult to see it when these sensations become more acute.
Nevertheless, there are special circumstances of heightened feeling, such as religious devotion and sexual passion, in which far more poignant types of pleasure and pain
lose their distinction. Ordinarily, such ascetic disciplines
as self-flagellation, wearing hair shirts, and kneeling on
chains are adopted to do violence to the desire for pleasure.
Yet it is possible that asceticism is a way of genuine spiritual insight because it leads eventually, however unintentionally, to the realization that in the ardor of devotion

pleasure and pain are a single ecstasy. Consider, for example, Bernini's celebrated effigy of St. Theresa of Ávila
in rapture, pierced by the dart of the divine love. The face
is equally expressive of ravishment or torture, and the smile
of the angel wielding the dart is accordingly compassionate
or cruel.

Perverse and abnormal as they are usually regarded, we
should also consider the phenomena of sadism and masochism—better designated by the single term algolagnia,
or "lustful pain." Merely to dismiss these phenomena as
perverse and unnatural is to say no more than that they
do not fit into a preconceived notion of order. The very
fact that they are human possibilities shows that they are
extensions of ordinary feelings, revealing depths of our
nature which are usually left unexplored. Distasteful as
they may be, this should not prevent us from trying to discover whether they throw any light on the problem of
suffering.

The sadist is really a vicarious masochist, for in inflict-
ing pain he identifies himself emotionally with his victim,
and gives a sexual interpretation to his victim's reactions
to pain. For masochism or algolagnia is the association of
the orgiastic convulsions of pain with sexual ecstasy, and
involves far more than that the two types of reaction look
somewhat alike to an external observer. The masochist
finds in pain of certain types a positive stimulant to sexual
orgasm, and as the intensity of his feeling increases he is
able to delight in harsher and harsher degrees of pain. The
standard Freudian explanation is that the masochist so
associates sexual pleasure with guilt that he cannot permit
himself this pleasure unless he is also being punished. This
seems to me to be doubtful and, like so much Freudian reasoning, unnecessarily complex, stretching facts to fit theories at all costs. For masochism is found in cultures where

sexuality and sin are not allied to anything like the degree to which they are wedded in the Christian West.[3] It would be simpler and more reasonable to say that the masochist intensifies or stimulates sexual reactions by inducing similar reactions arising from pain. To this it should be added that the masochist's desire to be subjugated or humiliated is allied to the fact that all sexual ecstasy, male or female, has a quality of self-abandonment, of surrender to a force greater than the ego.

A still more notable instance of the pleasure-pain identity has come to light in the work of the British obstetrician Grantley Dick Reid in his remarkably successful techniques of natural childbirth. Labor pains may ordinarily reach a degree of extreme severity so as to reach almost the highest level of pain which the organism can experience. The interest of Reid's technique is that it focuses the mother's attention on the feeling of the uterine contraction itself, dissociating it from socially implanted ideas of how it is supposed to feel. So long as she regards it as a pain she will resist it, but if she can approach it simply as a tension she can be shown how to go with it and relax into it—a technique which is learned through prenatal exercises. By thus abandoning herself without reserve to the spontaneous contractions of the uterus, she can experience childbirth as an extremely strong physical ecstasy rather than a torture.

Now it may appear that all these types of pleasure-pain are induced hypnotically, through the circumstances of religious devotion, sexual passion, or the physician's authoritative suggestions. To some extent this is perhaps true, although it might be better to call it a counterhypnotism,

[3] There is some evidence to show that deliberate masochism was first introduced into the West from Arabian culture—a culture notably free from sexual squeamishness. See Havelock Ellis (1), Part II, p. 130, quoting Eulenburg, *Sadismus und Masochismus.*

counter, that is, to the immense force of social suggestion which has taught us since babyhood how we ought to interpret our sensations and feelings. Surely the child learns much of how he should experience his sensations of pain from the attitudes of sympathy, horror, or disgust displayed by his parents. In these attitudes the child sees sympathetic resistances to pain which he learns to make for himself.

On the other hand, circumstances of religious ardor, sexual passion, or medical assurance create an atmosphere in which the organism can permit its own spontaneous reactions to the full. Under these conditions the organism is no longer split into the natural animal and the controlling ego. The whole being is one with its own spontaneity and feels free to let go with the utmost abandon. The same conditions are induced by such religious exercises as the dervish dance or the chanting of *mantrams*, the rites of the Penitentes or the glossolalia (tongue-blabbering) of Pentecostal preachers. But the frantic, explosive, and even dangerous character of some of these abandonments to spontaneity is largely the result of its normal restraint. In a culture where sex is calculated, religion decorous, dancing polite, music refined or sentimental, and yielding to pain shameful, many people have never experienced full spontaneity. Little or nothing is known of its integrating, cathartic, and purifying consequences, let alone of the fact that it may not only be creatively controlled, but also become a constant way of life. Under such circumstances the cultivation of spontaneity is left to the "social underground" of Negro revivals, jam sessions, or rock-and-roll parties. We cannot even conceive that Coomaraswamy's description of the sage as living "a perpetual uncalculated life in the present" [4] could mean anything but total disorder.

[4] A. K. Coomaraswamy (1), p. 134.

The point here, however, is that when the organism's natural reactions to pain are permitted without restraint, pain goes beyond pleasure and pain to ecstasy, which is really the proper equivalent of *ananda*. We begin here to find an approach to the mystery of human suffering which is adequate to the immense inevitability of the problem. This is not to say that our efforts to reduce the amount of pain in the world should be given up, but only that at best they are pitifully insufficient. The same insufficiency affects all the ordinary religious and philosophical rationalizations, wherein suffering is somehow explained away as a temporary means in the fulfillment of a divine plan or as a penalty for sin or as an illusion of the finite mind. One feels almost instinctively that some of these answers are an affront to the *dignity* of suffering and to its overwhelming reality for every single form of life. For as we look back and forward into the history of the universe we find little evidence and little assurance of orderly comfort as anything but a rarity. Life has been and looks as if it will be for the most part convulsive and catastrophic, maintaining itself by slaying and eating itself.[5] The problem of suffering will therefore continue to have a kind of awesome holiness so long as life depends in any way upon the pain of even a single creature.

One must respect the Indian ideal of *ahimsa* or "harmlessness" and the Buddhist monk's reduction of killing and causing pain to the utmost minimum. But in effect this abstinence is no more than a gesture which, when we really come down to it, is a retreat from the problem. Again, the answer to the problem of suffering is not away from the

[5] It is curious to speculate upon the consequences of civilized man's refusal to be eaten by other forms of life, to return his body for the fertilization of the soil from which he took it. This is a significant symptom of his alienation from nature, and may be a by no means negligible deprivation of the earth's resources.

problem but in it. The inevitability of pain will not be met by deadening sensitivity but by increasing it, by exploring and feeling out the manner in which the natural organism itself wants to react and which its innate wisdom has provided. The physician attending the deathbed will have to use the same means as the physician attending childbed, creating an atmosphere in which the physical or moral revulsions to death and its pains are fully permitted and encouraged. The feelings of a suffering being must be allowed to move unblocked as nature directs them, subject only to the external control of destructive action.

We begin to see, then, that the *answer* to suffering is the organism's *response* to it, its innate tendency to transmute unavoidable pain into ecstasy. This is the insight which underlies the cosmological myth of Hinduism, where the world in all the fullness of its delight and horror is seen as the ecstasy of God, perpetually incarnating himself by an act of self-abandonment in the myriad forms of creatures. This is why Shiva, the divine prototype of all suffering and destruction, is *Nataraja*, the "Lord of the Dance." For the everlasting, agonizing dissolution and renewal of life is the dance of Shiva, always ecstatic because it is without inner conflict, because in other words it is nondual— without the resistance of a controller external to the controlled, without any other principle of motion than its own *sahaja*, or spontaneity.

Left thus to itself, the spontaneity of the organism encounters no obstacle to its continued movement, which, like flowing water, perpetually finds out the course of least resistance, for as Lao-tzu said:

> The highest goodness is like water. Water is beneficent to all things but does not contend. It stays in [lowly] places which others despise. Therefore it is near Tao.[6] *viii*

[6] Ch'u Ta-kao (1), p. 18.

Because it does not block itself, the course of feeling acquires a sensation of freedom or "voidness," represented in Buddhist and Taoist terminology as *wu-hsin*—that is, "egolessness" or "no-mindness"—no feeler in conflict with feeling. In sorrow as in joy, in pain as in pleasure, the natural reactions follow one another without hindrance "like a ball in a mountain stream."

Suffering and death—all that dark and destructive side of nature for which Shiva stands—are therefore problematic for the ego rather than the organism. The organism accepts them through ecstasy, but the ego is rigid and unyielding and finds them problematic because they affront its pride. For, as Trigant Burrow has shown, the ego is the social image or role with which the mind is shamed into identifying itself, since we are taught to act the part which society wants us to play—the part of a reliable and predictable center of action which resists spontaneous change. But in extreme suffering and in death this part cannot be played, and as a result they become associated with all the shame and fear with which, as children, we were forced into becoming acceptable egos. Death and agony are therefore dreaded as loss of status, and their struggles are desperate attempts to maintain the assumed patterns of action and feeling. Yet in some traditional societies the individual prepares for death by abandoning status before he dies, that is, by relinquishing his role or caste and becoming, with full social approval, a "nobody." In practice, however, this is often frustrated by the fact that being "nobody" becomes a new kind of status—the formal role of "holy man" or *sanyassin,* the conventionally ecclesiastical monk.

The fear of spontaneity from which this arises is based not only on the confusion of the natural and biological type of order with the political, with legal and enforced order.

It arises also from failure to see that the socially problematic spontaneity of little children is as yet unco-or-
dinated and "embryonic." We then make the mistake of
socializing children, not by developing their spontaneity,
but by developing a system of resistances and fears which,
as it were, splits the organism into a spontaneous center
and an inhibiting center. Thus it is rare indeed to find an
integrated person capable of self-controlling spontaneity,
which sounds like a contradiction in terms. It is as if we
were teaching our children to walk by lifting up their feet
with their own hands instead of moving their legs from
within. We do not see that before spontaneity can control itself it must be able to function. The legs must have
full freedom of movement before they can acquire the discipline of walking and running or dancing. For disciplined
motion is the control of relaxed motion. Similarly, disciplined action and feeling is the direction of relaxed action
and feeling to prearranged ends. The pianist must therefore acquire relaxation and freedom in his arms and fingers
before he can execute complex musical figures, but much
abominable technique has been acquired by forcing the
fingers to perform piano exercises without preliminary
relaxation.[7]

Spontaneity is, after all, total sincerity—the whole being involved in the act without the slightest reservation—
and as a rule the civilized adult is goaded into it only by
abject despair, intolerable suffering, or imminent death.
Hence the proverb, "Man's extremity is God's opportun-
ity." Thus a modern Hindu sage has remarked that the first
thing he has to teach Westerners who come to him is how
to cry, which also goes to show that our spontaneity is

[7] See L. Bonpensiere (1). It is true that Beethoven fingered certain
passages in his sonatas in such a way that they could be played only with
a feeling of strain and conflict, but this is merely the exception that
proves the rule. He wanted these passages to express conflict musically.

inhibited not only by the ego-complex as such but also by
the Anglo-Saxon conception of masculinity. So far from
being a form of strength, the masculine rigidity and tough-
ness which we affect is nothing more than an emotional
paralysis. It is assumed not because we are in control of
our feelings but because we fear them, along with everything in our nature that is symbolically feminine and yielding. But a man who is emotionally paralyzed cannot be
male, that is, he cannot be male in relation to female, for
if he is to relate himself to a woman there must be something of the woman in his nature.

He who knows the masculine and yet keeps to the feminine
Will become a channel drawing all the world towards it;
Being a channel for the world, he will not be severed from
    the eternal virtue,
And then he can return again to the state of infancy (i.e.,
    to spontaneity).[8] xxviii

Childlikeness, or artless simplicity, is the ideal of the
artist no less than of the sage, for it is to perform the work
of art or of life without the least trace of affectation, of
being in two minds. But the way to the child is through
the woman, through yielding to spontaneity, through giving in to just what one is, moment by moment, in the
ceaselessly changing course of nature. It is to this "just
what one is" that the Hindu adage *Tat tvam asi*—"That
art thou"—refers, and *That* is the eternal, nondual Brahman. To the degree, however, that this way is not one of
anxiety-ridden self-control, it is equally removed from the
exhibitionism of the arty libertine whose display of "being
himself" is designed to shock and draw attention. His
vices are as hypocritical as a Pharisee's virtues. I remember
an *avant-garde* party at which a number of young men

[8] Ch'u Ta-kao (1), p. 38.

wandering around stark naked were more fully clothed than anyone else in the room, failing to realize that nakedness is a state that we cannot avoid. For our clothes, our skins, our personalities, our virtues and our vices are as transparent as space. We cannot lay claim to them, and there is no one to lay the claim, since the self is as transparent as its garments.

Empty and nihilistic as it may sound, this recognition of total nakedness and transparency is a joy beyond all telling, for what is empty is not reality itself but all that seems to block its light.

> Old P'ang requires nothing in the world:
> All is empty with him, even a seat he has not,
> For absolute Emptiness reigns in his household;
> How empty indeed it is with no treasures!
> When the sun is risen, he walks through Emptiness,
> When the sun sets, he sleeps in Emptiness;
> Sitting in Emptiness he sings his empty songs,
> And his empty songs reverberate through Emptiness.[9]

To name or symbolize the joyous content of this emptiness is always to say too much, to put, as they say in Zen, legs upon the snake. For in Buddhist philosophy emptiness (*sunyata*) denotes the most solid and basic reality, though it is called empty because it never becomes an *object* of knowledge. This is because, being common to all related terms—figure and ground, solid and space, motion and rest —it is never seen in contrast with anything else and thus is never seen as an object. It may be called the fundamental reality or substance of the world only by analogy, for strictly speaking reality is known by contrast with unreality, and substance or stuff by contrast with shape or with empty space. However, it may be realized by the

---

[9] P'ang Chü-shih, ninth-century Zen master. In Suzuki (1), vol. 2, p. 297.

intuitive wisdom which Buddhists call *prajna,* for, as we have seen, it is really obvious that all related terms have an "inner identity" which, not being one of the terms, is in the true sense of the word "interminable"—unable to be described or imagined. For *prajna* is the mode of knowledge which is direct, which is not knowledge *in terms* of words, symbols, images, and logical classes with their inevitable duality of inside and outside.

The "emptiness" of the universe also signifies the fact that the outlines, forms, and boundaries to which we attach all terms are in constant change, and in this sense its reality cannot be fixed or limited. It is called empty because it cannot be grasped, for even

> the hills are shadows,
> And they flow from form to form,
> And nothing stands.

Yet all man's resistance to Shiva, to change, suffering, dissolution, and death, is a resistance to being transparent, even though the resistance itself is as a phantom hand clutching at clouds. Suffering is ultimately ecstasy because it pries loose our strangling grasp upon ourselves and melts "this all too solid flesh." For the everlasting renewal and dissolution of the world is the most emphatic and inescapable revelation of the fact that "form is emptiness, and emptiness itself is form," and that the agonized ego is a ring of defense around nothing. The transience from which we seek liberation is the very liberator.

There are no means or methods for understanding this, for every such device is artfulness, is ultimately an attempt to become something, to be more than this melting moment which the utmost tension of the will cannot hold. Belief in an unchanging God, an immortal soul, or even in a deathless nirvana as something to be gained is all part of this artfulness, as is equally the sterile certainty and aggressive cocksureness of atheism and scientific materialism. There is no way to where we are, and whoever seeks one finds only a slick wall of granite without passage or foothold. Yogas, prayers, therapies, and spiritual exercises are at root only elaborate postponements of the recognition that there is nothing to be grasped and no way to grasp it.

This is not to say that there is no God or to deny the possibility that there is some form of personal continuity beyond death. It is rather to say that a God to be grasped or believed in is no God, and that a continuity to be wished for is only a continuity of bondage. Death presents itself to us as the possibility of sleep without waking, or at most as the possibility of waking up as someone else altogether —just as we did when we were born. Depressing or frightening as it may appear at first sight, the thought of sleep without waking—ever—is strangely fruitful, since it works

To tease us out of thought, as doth eternity.

Such a contemplation of death renders the hard core of "I-ness" already insubstantial, the more so as we go into it thoroughly and see that sleep without waking is not to be confused with the fantasy of being shut up forever in darkness. It is the disappearance even of darkness, reducing the imagination to impotence and thought to silence. At this point we ordinarily busy our brains with other matters, but the fascination of the certainty of death can sometimes hold us wonder-struck until the moment of a curious illumination in which we see that what dies is not consciousness but memory. Consciousness recurs in every newborn creature, and wherever it recurs it is "I." And in so far as it is only *this* "I," it struggles again and again in hundreds of millions of beings against the dissolution which would set it free. To see this is to feel the most peculiar solidarity—almost identity—with other creatures, and to begin to understand the meaning of compassion.

In the intense joy which attends the full realization that we are momentary and transparent, and that nothing can be grasped, there is no question of an icy detachment from the world. A man who had realized this very fully once wrote to me, "I am now becoming as deeply attached as I can be to as many people and things as possible." For after the *pralaya* in which all the manifested worlds are dissolved, Brahma once again precipitates himself into the myriad forms of life and consciousness, and after he has realized nirvana, the Bodhisattva returns into the interminable round of birth-and-death.

> Even beyond the ultimate limits there extends a passage-
> way
> Whereby he comes back among the six realms of exist-
> ence. . . .
> Like a gem he stands out even in the mud;
> Like pure gold he shines even in the furnace.[10]

In attachment there is pain, and in pain deliverance, so that at this point attachment itself offers no obstacle, and the liberated one is at last free to love with all his might and to suffer with all his heart. This is not because he has learned the trick of splitting himself into higher and lower selves so that he can watch himself with inward indifference, but rather because he has found the meeting-point of the limit of wisdom and the limit of foolishness. The Bodhisattva is the fool who has become wise by persisting in his folly.

The well-intentioned reverence of innumerable believers has, of course, set the Buddhas, the sages, the liberated ones upon the summit of spiritual success, though by this

[10] Tzu-te Hui. In Suzuki (2), pp. 150–51.

means they have piously postponed their own awakening. For the realm of liberation is absolutely incommensurable with the relativities of higher and lower, better and worse, gain and loss, since these are all the transparent and empty advantages and disadvantages of the ego. Though not strictly accurate, it is less misleading to think of liberation as the depth of spiritual failure—where one cannot even lay claim to vices, let alone virtues. For in seeing fully into his own empty momentariness, the Bodhisattva knows a despair beyond suicide, the *absolute* despair which is the etymological meaning of nirvana. It is complete disillusion from every hope of safety, or rest, or gain, suicide itself being no escape since "I" awakens once more in every being that is born. It is the recognition of final defeat for all the artfulness of the ego, which, in this disillusion, expires— finding only emptiness in its most frantic resistance to emptiness, suffering in escape from suffering, and nothing but clinging in its efforts to let go. But here he finds in his own dissolving the same emptiness from which there blazes the whole host of sun, moon, and stars.

5: The World as Non-Sense

THAT OUR LIFE IS A DISSOLVING MOMENT IN which there is nothing to grasp and no one to grasp it is the negative way of saying something which may also be said positively. But the positive way is not quite so effective and forceful, and lends itself more easily to misunderstanding. The sense that there is something to be grasped rests upon the seeming duality of the ego and its experience. But the reason why there is nothing to be grasped is that this duality is only seeming, so that the attempt to cling is like trying to bite the teeth with the teeth, or to clutch the hand with the hand. The corollary of this realization is that subject and object, oneself and the world, are a unity or, to be precise, a "nonduality" since the word "unity" may be taken to exclude diversity.

The sense of the vast gulf between the ego and the world disappears, and one's subjective, inner life seems no longer to be separate from everything else, from one's total experience of the stream of nature. It becomes simply obvious that "everything is the Tao"—an integrated, harmonious, and universal process from which it is absolutely impossible to deviate. This sensation is marvellous, to put it mildly, though there is no logical reason why it should be so, unless it is just through release from the chronic feeling of having to "face" reality. For here one does not face life any more; one simply is it.

But things are not usually felt to be marvellous unless they are full of consequence, unless they lead to definitive changes in practical life. When this sensation first dawns upon people, as it often does quite unexpectedly, they are apt to expect all kinds of results from it, which is why it vanishes as swiftly as it comes. They expect it to change their characters, to make them better, stronger, wiser, and happier. For they believe that they have grasped something immensely valuable, and go bouncing around as if they had inherited a fortune.

A Zen master was once asked, "What is the most valuable thing in the world?" He answered, "The head of a dead cat!" "Why?" "Because no one can put a price on it." The realization of the unity of the world is like this dead cat's head. It is the most priceless, the most inconsequential thing of all. It has no results, no implications, and no logical meaning. One cannot get anything out of it because it is impossible to take up a position outside it from which to reach in and grasp. The whole notion of gain, whether it be the gain of wealth or the gain of knowledge and virtue, is like stopping the pangs of hunger by gobbling oneself up from the toes. Yet we do it anyhow, for it really makes no difference whether it is one's own toes or roast duck: the satisfaction is always momentary. As the *Upanishads* say, *"Annam Brahman*—food is Brahman. I, the food, eat the eater of food!" [1] We are all eating ourselves like the serpent Ouroboros, and the only real disappointment comes from expecting to get something from it. This is why the Buddha said to his disciple Subhuti, "I gained absolutely nothing from unsurpassed and perfect Awakening." On the other hand, when there is no expectation, no looking for a result, and nothing gained but this "head of a dead cat," there is quite suddenly and gratuitously, quite miraculously and unreasonably, more than one ever had sought.

This is not a matter of renunciation and repressing desire

[1] *Taittiriya Upanishad, iii,* 10, 6.

—those traps which the clever and cunning lay for God. One cannot renounce life for the same reason that one cannot gain from it. As is said in the *Cheng-tao Ke*:

> *You cannot take hold of it,*
> *But you cannot lose it.*
> *In not being able to get it, you get it.*
> *When you are silent, it speaks;*
> *When you speak, it is silent.* xxxiv

For although it is often said that to seek the Tao is to lose it, since seeking puts a gap between the seeker and the sought, this is not quite true, as becomes evident when we try compulsively not to seek, not to wish, not to cling. The truth, however, is that one cannot deviate from the Tao even by seeking for it. There simply is no wrong attitude to the Tao because, again, there is no point outside it from which to take an attitude. The seeming separation of the subjective self is just as much an expression of the Tao as the clear outline of a leaf.

Such assertions will naturally be irritating to sensible and practical minds—this excitement about something which does not necessarily make any difference to anything, this perfectly meaningless idea of a harmony from which it is impossible to deviate. But the whole point of this "dead cat's head" philosophy is just that it is inconsequential, that, like nature itself, it is a kind of sublime nonsense, an expression of ecstasy, an end in itself without purpose or goal.

Restless, probing, and grasping minds are completely frustrated by such pointlessness, since for them only that has meaning which, like a word, points to something beyond itself. Therefore in so far as the world seems meaningful to them they have reduced it to a collection of signs like a dictionary. In their world flowers have scent and color *in order* to attract bees, and chameleons change their skin-tone with the intent of concealing themselves. Or, if what they are projecting upon nature is not mind but machinery, bees are attracted to flowers because they have scent and color, and chameleons survive because they have skin which changes its tone. They do not see the world of color and scented bee-visited flowers growing—without the abstract and divisive "because." Instead of interrelated patterns wherein all the parts grow simultaneously together, they see conglomerations of "billiard ball" things, strung together by the temporal sequence of cause and effect. In such a world things are what they are only in relation to what was and what will be, but in the goalless world of the Tao, things are what they are in relation to each other's *presence*.

Perhaps we may now begin to see why men have an almost universal tendency to seek relief from their own kind among the trees and plants, the mountains and waters. There is an easy and rather cheap sophistication in mocking the love of nature, but there is always something profound and essential in the universal theme of poetry, however hackneyed. For hundreds of years the great poets of East and West have given expression to this basically human love of "communing with nature," a phrase which in present-day intellectual circles seems to have acquired a slightly ridiculous tone. Presumably it is regarded as one of those "escapes from reality" so much condemned by those who restrict reality to what one reads about in the newspapers.

But perhaps the reason for this love of nonhuman nature is that communion with it restores us to a level of our own human nature at which we are still sane, free from humbug, and untouched by anxieties about the meaning and purpose of our lives. For what we call "nature" is free from a certain kind of scheming and self-importance. The birds and beasts indeed pursue their business of eating and breeding with the utmost devotion. But they do not justify it; they do not pretend that it serves higher ends, or that it makes a significant contribution to the progress of the world.

This is not meant to sound unkind to human beings, because the point is not so simple as that the birds are right and we are wrong. The point is that rapport with the marvellously purposeless world of nature gives us new eyes for ourselves—eyes in which our very self-importance is not condemned, but seen as something quite other than what it imagines itself to be. In this light all the weirdly abstract and pompous pursuits of men are suddenly transformed into natural marvels of the same order as the immense beaks of the toucans and hornbills, the fabulous tails of the birds of paradise, the towering necks of the giraffes, and the vividly polychromed posteriors of the baboons. Seen thus, neither as something to be condemned nor in its accustomed aspect of serious worth, the self-importance of man dissolves in laughter. His insistent purposefulness and his extraordinary preoccupation with abstractions are, while perfectly natural, overdone—like the vast bodies of the dinosaurs. As means of survival and adaptation they have been overplayed, producing a species too cunning and too practical for its own good, and which for this very reason stands in need of the "dead cat's head" philosophy. For this is the philosophy which, like nature, has no purpose or consequence other than itself.

Yet by indirection, surprisingly and artlessly, this philosophy arrives at an immensely heightened perception of the significance of the world. Perhaps "significance" is the wrong word, for seen thus the world does not point to a meaning beyond itself. It is like pure music—music when

it is not a support for words, when it is not imitating natural
sounds, and when, we might almost say, it does not represent feeling but *is* feeling. It is like the poetry of incanta-
tion and spellbinding where the words themselves are the
meaning—

> *The silver is white, red is the gold;*
> *The robes they lay in fold.*
> *The bailey beareth the bell away;*
> *The lily, the rose, the rose I lay.*

People who turn with incomprehension from a nonobjec-
tive painting will nevertheless gaze with delight at a landscape where the artist has represented clouds and rocks
which themselves represent nothing, paying unconscious
tribute to the wonder of natural nonsense. For it is not as
if these forms moved us by their approximation to the intelligible shapes of the geometer or by their resemblance to
other things; the clouds are no less beautiful when not
reminding us of mountains and cities in the sky. The rush
of waterfalls and the babbling of streams are not loved for
their resemblance to speech; the irregularly scattered stars
do not excite us because of the formal constellations which
have been traced out between them; and it is for no sym-
metry or suggestion of pictures that we delight in the patterns of foam, of the veins in rock, or of the black branches
of trees in wintertime.

Seen in this light, the bewildering complexity of nature
is a dance with no destination other than the figures now in
performance, figures improvised not in response to an over-
ruling law but mutually to each other. Even the cities lose
their calculated practicality and become pumping ganglia
in a network of arteries spread over the earth, sucking their
corpuscles in at dawn and spitting them out at sunset.
Caught up in the illusion of time and teleology, the dance

and the ecstatic rhythm of the process is hidden and is seen instead as a frenzied pursuit, fighting its way through delays and obstacles. But when the final futility of the pursuit is recognized, the mind comes to rest and notices the rhythm, becoming aware that the timeless intent of the process is fulfilled at each instant.

There are occasions when this vision of the world takes us by surprise, the mind having slipped unconsciously into a receptive attitude. It is like the oft-recurring tale of coming upon an unexpected door in a familiar wall, a door that leads into an enchanted garden, or a cleft in a rock that gives entrance to a cavern of jewels. Yet when one comes back to the place again, looking for the entrance, it is no longer to be found. It was in just this way that late one afternoon my own garden became suddenly transfigured— for about half an hour, just at the beginning of twilight. The sky was in some way transparent, its blue quiet and clear, but more inwardly luminous than ever at high noon. The leaves of the trees and shrubs assumed qualities of green that were incandescent, and their clusterings were no longer shapeless daubs, but arabesques of marvellous complexity and clarity. The interlacing of branches against the sky suggested filigree or tracery, not in the sense of artificiality, but of distinctness and rhythm. Flowers—I remember especially the fuchsias—were suddenly the lightest carvings of ivory and coral.

It is as if the impressions of a restless and seeking mind are blurred by the speed at which they are overpassed, so that the rhythmic clarity of forms is unnoticed, and colors are seen flat without inner light. Furthermore, it is characteristic of almost all these openings of vision that every detail of the world appears to be in order, not as on a parade ground but as perfectly interconnected with everything else so that nothing is irrelevant, nothing inessential.

This, perhaps more than anything, explains the logically nonsensical feeling that everything is "right," or in harmony with the Tao, just as it is. And this applies equally to impressions that would ordinarily be thought simply messy, like garbage in a gutter or a spilled ash-tray on the carpet . . . or the head of a dead cat.

In the Western world it is second nature for us to assume that all creative action requires the incentive of inadequacy and discontent. It seems obvious that if we felt fulfilled at each instant and no longer regarded time as a path of pursuit, we should just sit down in the sun, pull large Mexican hats over our eyes, and put bottles of tequila at our elbows. Even if this were true it might not be so great a disaster as we imagine, for there is no doubt that our extreme busyness is as much nervous fidgets as industry, and that a certain amount of ordinary laziness would lend our culture the pleasant mellowness which it singularly lacks. However, it does not seem to occur to us that action goaded by a sense of inadequacy will be creative only in a limited sense. It will express the emptiness from which it springs rather than fullness, hunger rather than strength. Thus when our love for others is based simply on mutual need it becomes strangling—a kind of vampirism in which we say, all too expressively, "I love you so much I could eat you!" It is from such desiring that parental devotion becomes smother-love and marriage holy deadlock.

Modern theologians have used the Greek words *eros* and *agape* to distinguish between hungering love and generous love, ascribing the latter, however, to God alone. The fallen nature of man can only hunger, because sin is a descent from the fullness of Being to Nothingness. Lacking divine grace, man can act only from the natural incentive of need, and this assumption persists as a matter of common sense even when it is no longer believed that there is a God creating the world out of his infinite fullness. We assume, furthermore, that the whole realm of nature acts from hunger alone, for in Christianity it was understood that nature fell together with Adam, its head. And the notion that nature acts only from necessity accords perfectly with the mechanism which displaces theism.

But if the Fall was the loss of our sense of integrity with nature, the supposedly hunger-driven quality of natural action is a projection upon the world of our own state. If we are to abandon Newtonian mechanics in the physical sphere we must also do so in the psychological and moral. In the same measure that the atoms are not billiard balls struck into motion by others, our actions are not entities forced into operation by distinct motives and drives. Actions appear to be forced by other things to the degree that the agent identifies himself with a single part of the situation in which the actions occur, such as the will as distinct from the passions, or the mind as distinct from the body. But if he identifies himself with his passions and with his body, he will not seem to be moved by them. If he can go further and see that he is not simply his body but the whole of his body-environment relationship, he will not even feel forced to act by the environment. The effect appears to be controlled passively by its cause only in so far as it is considered to be distinct from the cause. But if cause and effect are just the terms of a single act, there is neither controller nor controlled. Thus the feeling that action has to spring from necessity comes from thinking that the self is the center of consciousness as distinct from the periphery.

The question "Why should one act?" has meaning only so long as motivation seems necessary to action. But if action or process rather than inert substance is what constitutes the world, it is absurd to seek an external reason for action. There is really no alternative to action, and this is not to say that we *must* act, since this would imply the reality of the inert, substantial "we" reluctantly activated from outside. The point is that, motivated or not, we *are* action. But when action is felt to be motivated, it expresses the hungering emptiness of the ego, the inertness of entity rather than the liveliness of act. When, however, man is not pursuing something outside himself, he is action expressing its own fullness, whether weeping for sorrow or jumping for joy.

In Indian philosophy *karma* signifies both motivated or purposeful action and cause and effect, and *karma* is the type of action which holds man in bondage. Goal-seeking, it reaches no goal, but ever perpetuates the need for goals. Solving problems, it ever creates more problems to solve. *Karma* is therefore significant action because, like the sign, it points beyond itself to a meaning, to the motive from which it sprang or the end which it seeks. It is action creating the *necessity* for further action. On the other hand, *sahaja* is spontaneous and inconsequential action characteristic of the *jivan-mukta*, the liberated one, who lives and moves in the same way as nature—babbling like streams, gesticulating like trees in the wind, wandering like clouds, or just existing like rocks on the sand. His life has the quality of what the Japanese call *fura-fura*— the flapping of a cloth in the breeze or the motion of an empty gourd in a bubbling river. "The wind bloweth where it listeth, and thou hearest the voice thereof, but canst not tell whence it cometh nor whither it goeth." No more can the wind itself.

This is why there is a universal likening of sages to lunatics, since in their subtly differing ways neither make any sense nor accept the world's practical scale of values.

His door stands closed, and the wise ones do not know him. His inner life is hidden, and he moves outside the ruts of the recognized virtues. Carrying a gourd, he enters the marketplace; making his way with a staff, he returns home. Even in the liquor shop and the fish market everyone is transformed into a Buddha.

Bare-chested and bare-footed, he goes into the dust of this world.
Smeared with mud and daubed with ashes, he wears a broad grin.
He has no need of the secret powers of the gods,
For by his direct command the dead trees blossom with flowers.[2]

For as the nonsense of the madman is a babble of words for its own fascination, the nonsense of nature and of the sage is the perception that the ultimate meaninglessness of the world contains the same hidden joy as its transience and emptiness. If we seek the meaning in the past, the chain of cause and effect vanishes like the wake of a ship. If we seek it in the future, it fades out like the beam of a searchlight in the night sky. If we seek it in the present, it is as elusive as flying spray, and there is nothing to grasp. But when only the seeking remains and we seek to know what *this* is, it suddenly turns into the mountains and waters, the sky and the stars, sufficient to themselves with no one left to seek anything from them.

*   *   *

From all that has been said until now it may seem that our philosophy of nature has reached a point of complete self-contradiction. For if what it comes to is that there is no real division between man and nature, it follows that

[2] *Shih Niu T'ou,* x. Comment on the last of the *Ten Oxherding Pictures* which illustrate the stages of realization in Zen Buddhism.

there is nothing artificial from which the natural can be distinguished. As Goethe said again in the *Fragment on Nature:*

> The most unnatural also is nature. Who sees her not on all sides sees her truly nowhere. . . . Even in resisting her laws one obeys them; and one works with her even in desiring to work against her.

If this be true it would seem to render null all that has been said about the mechanical and unnatural character of the monotheistic God and of the linear and political views of the world order shared by Christianity and, until recently, by the philosophy of science. It would also seem to be pointless to prefer one mode of consciousness to another, to consider the open attentiveness of *kuan* more natural than the straining and staring attitude of egocentricity. If even the self-conscious artificialities and conceits of urban and industrial civilization are no more unnatural than the pretentious tail feathers of the peacock, this amounts to saying that in the natural life anything and everything "goes." As we said, there is no possibility of deviation from the Tao.

However, at the very least there is this much difference between such a position as this and, say, Christianity or a legalistic science: that they make a distinction between man and nature which this philosophy does not. It is granted that the making of this distinction is no less within the realm of nature than not making it. Both positions are therefore in some sense "right," if this is what we mean by natural, in the sense, perhaps, of a libertarian saying to a totalitarian, "I disagree entirely with what you say, but I will defend to the death your *right* to say it." As in an ideal democracy the exercise of freedom involves the right to vote for restrictions on freedom, so man's participation in nature involves the right and the freedom to feel that he stands above nature. As by democratic process the people may freely renounce freedom, one may likewise be naturally unnatural. Whereas the totalitarian may then assert that freedom has been abolished, the libertarian will point out that this is true only to the extent that he freely asserts it. Even under tyranny "a people gets what government it deserves," because it always retains the power, that is, the freedom to govern itself. In the same way it is possible for this philosophy to assert quite meaningfully that it is perfectly natural to believe that man is apart from nature and yet to disagree with the belief.

But if a people votes freely for certain restrictions on its freedom, it should never forget that freedom remains the background and authority for law. Similarly, the ultimate point of this philosophy is that as a people can never abandon its freedom and responsibility absolutely, a human being cannot absolutely abandon his naturalness and, likewise, should never forget it. To put it in another way, naturalness is a self-determining spontaneity (*tzu-jan*) which we retain even in the most awkward rigidity and affectation of attitude. But the "we" which retains this spontaneity is not the self-restriction called "ego"; it is the natural man, the organism-environment relationship.

Thus if political health consists in realizing that legal restraint is freely self-imposed by the people, philosophical health consists in realizing that our true self is the natural man, the spontaneous Tao, from which we never deviate. In psychological terms this realization is a total self-acceptance standing, like political freedom, as the constant background of every thought, feeling, and action—however restricted. Such acceptance of oneself is the condition of that underlying integrity, sincerity, and peace of heart which, in the sage, endures beneath every disturbance. It

is, in short, a deeply inward consent to be just exactly what
we are and to feel just exactly what we are feeling at every
moment, even before what we are has been changed, however slightly, by accepting it. It is the recognition that "all
things are lawful for me," even if "not all are expedient,"
but probably in a far wider sense than St. Paul ever intended. Stated boldly, if crudely, it is the insight that whatever we are just now, that is now what we should ideally
be. This is the sense of the Zen Buddhist saying, "Your ordinary mind is the Tao," the "ordinary mind" being the present, given state of consciousness, whatever its nature. For
enlightenment, or accord with the Tao, remains unrealized
so long as it is considered as a specific state to be attained,
and for which there are tests and standards of success. It
is much rather freedom to be the failure that one is.

Unlikely as it may seem, this outrageous and nonmoral
freedom is the basis of all mental and spiritual wholeness,
provided, I was about to say, that it seeks no result. But so
full an acceptance includes also this seeking, along with
just anything that one happens to be doing or feeling. The
apparently extreme passivity of this acceptance is, however, creative because it permits one to be all of a piece,
to be good, bad, indifferent, or merely confused, with a
whole heart. To act or grow creatively we must begin from
where we are, but we cannot begin at all if we are not
"all here" without reservation or regret. Lacking self-
acceptance, we are always at odds with our point of de-
parture, always doubting the ground on which we stand,
always so divided against ourselves that we cannot act
with sincerity. Apart from self-acceptance as the groundwork of thought and action, every attempt at spiritual or
moral discipline is the fruitless struggle of a mind that is
split asunder and insincere. It is the freedom which is the
essential basis of self-restraint.

In the West we have always admitted in theory that truly moral acts must be expressions of freedom. Yet we have never allowed this freedom, never permitted ourselves to be everything that we are, to see that fundamentally all the gains and losses, rights and wrongs of our lives are as natural and "perfect" as the peaks and valleys of a mountain range. For in identifying God, the Absolute, with a goodness excluding evil we make it impossible for us to accept ourselves radically: what is not in accord with the will of God is at variance with Being itself and must not under any circumstances be accepted. Our freedom is therefore set about with such catastrophic rewards and punishments that it is not freedom at all, but resembles rather the totalitarian state in which one *may* vote against the government but always at the risk of being sent to a concentration camp. Instead of self-acceptance, the groundwork of our thought and action has therefore been metaphysical anxiety, the terror of being ultimately wrong and rotten to the core.

It is for this reason that the formal Catholic and Protestant orthodoxies have always been strictly exoteric doctrines, identifying the Absolute with the relativities of good and evil. Theologians are wont to say that if the distinctions between good and evil are not valid eternally they are not truly valid and important distinctions. But this actually amounts to saying that what is finite and relative is not important—a strange view for those who also insist that there is a real finite creation distinct from God and an object of his love. Not to be able to distinguish the absolutely important from the relatively important without thinking the latter unimportant is surely to adopt a most primitive scale of values.

Conversely, there is always the risk that a fundamental self-acceptance will render a person insensitive to the im-

portance of moral values, but this is only to say that without risk there is no freedom. The fear that self-acceptance
necessarily annihilates ethical judgment is groundless, for
we are perfectly able to distinguish between up and down
at any point on the earth's surface, realizing at the same
time that there is no up and down in the larger framework
of the cosmos. Self-acceptance is therefore the spiritual and
psychological equivalent of space, of a freedom which does
not annihilate distinctions but makes them possible.

> The capacity of the mind is great, like the emptiness of
> space. . . . The marvelous nature of the ordinary person is
> fundamentally empty and has no fixed character. Such is
> the truly sky-like quality of one's natural self. . . . The
> emptiness of universal space can contain the myriad things
> of every shape and form—the sun, moon, and stars, the
> mountains and rivers, the great earth with its springs,
> streams, and waterfalls, grass, trees, and dense forests, its
> sinners and saints, and the ways of good and evil. . . . All
> these are in the void, and the ordinary person's nature is
> void in just this way.[3]

But the healing and liberating force of self-acceptance
is so contrary to the expectations of our pedestrian common
sense that its power seems almost uncanny even to the psy-
chotherapist who watches it happen again and again. For
it is just this which restores the integrity and responsibility
of the sick mind, liberating it from every radical compulsion to be what it is not. Nevertheless, this emergence of
law from liberty, of cosmos from the void, and of energy
from passivity is always so miraculously unexpected and
improbable that it does not ordinarily come about except
by some stratagem which enables us to permit ourselves
this freedom in such a way that the right hand does not
know what the left is doing. Thus we can bring ourselves

[3] Hui-neng, eighth-century Zen master, in the *Tan-ching, ii.*

to self-acceptance vicariously, through the agency of a liberalized God who is infinitely loving and forgiving, so that
it is *he* who accepts us totally, and not, at least directly, we
ourselves. Or it may be that we can accord ourselves the
right to self-acceptance only when we have paid for it by
going through some disciplinary mill or spiritual obstacle-
course, whereafter our acceptance of ourselves is rein-
forced by the collective authority of fellow initiates, representing some hallowed tradition.[4] Such are the ways of
placating the fear of freedom which society must almost
inevitably implant from our childhood. For lacking dis-
crimination between the hierarchies of value and truth, the
child may say that two and two are five if he is told the
higher mathematical truth that they are not always and
necessarily four.

Growth in philosophical understanding, or just plain
wisdom, is always a matter of being able to distinguish between levels of truth and frames of reference, at the same
time being able to see one's own life in its intimate relation
to these differing and ever more universal levels. Above all,
there is the level beyond levels, the boundless frame of
universal nature, which, however impossible to describe, is
the self-determining and spontaneous ground of our being
and our freedom. The degree of our freedom and self-
determination varies with the level which we realize to be
our self—the source from which we act. As our sense of
self is narrow, the more we feel our existence as restraint.

[4] In the course of such preliminary disciplines the neophyte may sometimes acquire various skills and powers or subtle traits of character and
manner which are subsequently understood as the signs of his liberation.
This is, however, a confusion of freedom with success in particular skills.
Thus an initiate who, in his preliminary training, learned to stand pain
without flinching may be unable to run a farm or build a house as well
as any ordinary neurotic. His response to pain may in fact prove nothing
more than that he has learned the trick of self-hypnosis, or managed to
lose his sensitivity.

"And therefore," said Ruysbroeck, "we must all found our lives upon a fathomless abyss"—so to discover that what we are is not what we are bound to be, but what we are free to be. For when we stand with our nature, seeing that there is nowhere to stand against it, we are at last able to move unmoved.

II: MAN AND WOMAN

6: Spirituality and Sexuality

THE DIVISION OF LIFE INTO THE HIGHER
and lower categories of spirit and nature usually goes hand
in hand with a symbolism in which spirit is male and nature
female. The resemblance was perhaps suggested by the
rains falling from heaven to fertilize the earth, the plant-
ing of seed in the ground, and the ripening of the fruit by
the warmth of the sun. To a considerable extent ancient
man reasoned in terms of such correspondences, and made
sense of his world by seeing analogies between one natural
process and another, analogies which were understood to
be actual relationships. The art of astrology, for example,
is the most complete monument to this way of reasoning,
based as it is upon the correspondences between the mac-
rocosm and the microcosm, the order of the stars and the
order of terrestrial affairs. In the words of the Hermetic
Emerald Tablet:

> *Heaven above, heaven below;*
> *Stars above, stars below.*
> *All that is over, under shall show.*
> *Happy who the riddle readeth!*

Unfortunately for those who search for consistent systems in ancient cosmology, it was always possible to read
the correspondences as well as the very orders of heaven
and earth in different ways. Heaven might be male and
earth female, but then it was equally possible to think of
space and the sky as an all-embracing womb in which the

139

universe had been brought to birth, for such is apparently the sense of the Egyptian sky goddess Nut. It is easy, however, for us to dismiss such ways of thinking as mere projection, as a confusion of objective nature with fantasies which it evokes from the human mind. Yet after all our own science is likewise a projection, though what it reads into nature is not a loosely knit system of poetic images but the highly exact and consistent structure of mathematics. Both are products of the human mind, and mathematics in particular may be developed indefinitely in the abstract as a pure creation of thought without reference to any external experience. But mathematics *works* because of its immense inner consistency and precision, serving thus as an admirable tool for measuring nature to suit the purposes which *we* have in mind. However, not all cultures have the same purposes, so that other ways of "reading" the world may serve equally well for ends which are as legitimate as ours, for there are no laws by which these ends may be judged apart from the very readings of the world which serve them.

Indeed, the world is not unlike a vast, shapeless Rorschach blot which we read according to our inner disposition, in such a way that our interpretations say far more about ourselves than about the blot. But whereas the psychologist has tried to develop a science to judge and compare the various interpretations of the Rorschach Test, there is as yet no supracultural science, no "metascience," whereby we can assess our differing interpretations of the cosmic Rorschach blot. Cultural anthropology, the nearest thing to this, suffers the defect of being thoroughly embedded in the conventions of Western science, of one particular way of interpreting the blot.

The importance of the correspondence between spirit and man and nature and woman is that it projects upon the world a disposition in which the members of several cultures, including our own, are still involved. It is a disposition in which the split between man and nature is related to a problematic attitude to sex, though like egg and hen it is doubtful which came first. It is perhaps best to treat them as arising mutually, each being symptomatic of the other.

The historical reasons for our problematic attitude to sexuality are so obscure that there are numerous contradictory theories to explain it. It seems useless, therefore, to try to decide between them in the present state of our knowledge. The problem may be discussed more profitably just by taking the attitude as given, and by considering its consequences and alternatives. The fact is that in some unknown way the female sex has become associated with the earthy aspect of human nature and with sexuality as such. The male sex could conceivably have been put in the same position, and there is no conclusive evidence that women are more desirous and provocative of sexual activity than men, or *vice versa*. These are almost certainly matters of cultural conditioning which do not explain how the culture itself came to be as it is. It seems plausible that the association of women with sexuality as such is a male point of view arising in cultures where the male is dominant, but this in turn may be not so much a cause of the attitude as one of its concurrent symptoms. It is, however, very possible that the attitude to women is rather more accidental than the attitude to sexuality, for we know that the male and the female alike can feel the sexual relationship to be a seduction, a danger, and a problem. But *why* they do so at any time may no longer be the reason for their having first done so, so that knowledge of historical causes may not of itself provide any solution to the problem.

Thus to say that man's relation to nature is in some sense parallel to his relation to woman is to speak symbolically.

The real parallel is the relation of the human being, male or female, to the sexual division of the species and to all that it involves. When, therefore, we shall speak loosely of the *reasons* for certain sexual attitudes, we shall not be speaking of fundamental historical causes, for these are, strictly speaking, prehistoric—not necessarily so much in point of time as in extent of knowledge. We shall be speaking of the reasons as they exist today, either as matters of open knowledge or as forms of unconscious conditioning. There is no clear evidence that we are unconsciously conditioned by events from the remote historical past, and we must therefore be most cautious in using the insights of psychoanalysis for reconstructing the history of cultures. Certainly we can trace the historical effects of Christian, Buddhist, or Hindu doctrines upon our sexual attitudes, but what lies behind these doctrines and the attitudes from which they arose remains conjectural and dim. Furthermore, it is always possible to argue not that we are conditioned *by* the past, but that we use the past to condition ourselves in the present, and for reasons which are not historical but deeply inward and unknown. For example, a physiologist does not need to call upon the whole history of living creatures to explain why a person is hungry. He explains it from the present state of the organism.[1]

Let us then say that in the Christian and post-Christian West we simply find ourselves in a culture where nature is called Mother Nature, where God is exclusively male, and where one of the common meanings of Woman or Women with the capital W is simply sex, whereas Man with the

---

[1] It is of interest that in the academic world only the more or less "effete" disciplines are studied by the historical method. Beginning courses in religion, philosophy, or "culture" are usually historical, but the history of mathematics, chemistry, or medicine is the concern of a few specialists only. The ordinary student begins at once to learn them from their *present* rudiments.

capital *M* means humanity in general. As part and parcel of this situation, as distinct from its historical explanation, we find that in the Indo-European language system the words *matter, materia,* and *meter* as well as *mother,* and its Latin and Greek forms *mater* and μήτηρ, are derived alike from the Sanskrit root *mā-* (*mātr-*), from which, in Sanskrit itself, come both *mātā* (mother) and *māyā* (the phenomenal world of nature). The meaning of the common root *mā-* is "to measure," thus giving *māyā* the sense of the world-as-measured, that is, as divided up into things, events, and categories. In contrast stands the world unmeasured, the infinite and undivided (*advaita*) Brahman, the supreme spiritual reality. While it can be pointed out that the Devil is *also* male, since as the angel Lucifer he is a pure spirit, it must be noted that his popular form is simply that of the god Pan— the lusty spirit of earth and fertility, the genius of natural beauty. Hell, his domain, lies downward in the heart of the earth, where all is dark, inward, and unconscious as distinct from the bright heavens above. The catalogue of popular images, figures of speech, and customs which associate spirit with the divine, the good, and the male and nature with the material, evil, sexual, and female could go on indefinitely.

But the heart of the matter begins to reveal itself when, considering nature in the Chinese sense of spontaneity (*tzu-jan*), we begin to realize that the opposition of spirit to both nature and sexuality is the opposition of the conscious will, of the ego, to that which it cannot control. If sexual abstinence is, as in so many spiritual traditions, the condition of enhanced consciousness, it is because consciousness as we know it is an act of restraint. The point comes out clearly in St. Augustine's discussion of the spontaneity of the sexual member:

Justly, too, these members themselves, being moved and restrained not at our will, but by a certain independent autocracy, so to speak, are called "shameful." Their condition was different before sin . . . because not yet did lust move those members without the will's consent. . . . But when [our first parents] were stripped of grace, that their disobedience might be punished by fit retribution, there began to be in the movement of their bodily members a shameless novelty which made nakedness indecent.[2]

This is clearly the reaction of one for whom the soul, the will, the spiritual part of man, is identified with that form of consciousness which we have seen to be a partial and exclusive mode of attention. It is the mode of attention which grasps and orders the world by seeing it as one-at-a-time things, excluding and ignoring the rest. For it is this which involves that straining of the mind which is also the sensation of willing and of being a separate, exclusive ego.

Shame is thus the accompaniment of the failure of concentrated attention and will which manifests itself not only in the spontaneity of sexual excitement, but also in crying, trembling, blushing, blanching, and so many other socially "shameful" reactions.[3] These reactions are ordinarily avoided by concentrating the attention elsewhere and so avoiding the shameful response, and thus the ascetic disciplinarian will overcome lust, not by pitting the will against it directly, but by attending resolutely to other matters.

Obviously, the sexual function is one of the most powerful manifestations of biological spontaneity, and thus more

---

[2] *De Civitate Dei*, xiv, 17. Tr. Dods (1), vol. 2, p. 33.
[3] Note the "double bind" involved in blushing. One blushes because of shame and is in turn ashamed to blush, and is thus left with no alternative but to be "covered with confusion." This is a mild example of the way in which, as Gregory Bateson (1) has shown, double-bind situations lead to the more serious "confusion" of insanity, and especially schizophrenia.

especially difficult for the will to control. The immediate reasons for controlling it vary from the belief that it saps virility, through proprietary rights upon women, to its association with a complex love relationship with one woman alone, to mention only a few. But these seem to be secondary to the fact that sexual restraint is a principal test of the strength of the ego, along with resistance to pain and regulation of the wanderings of thought and feeling. Such restraints are the very substance of individual consciousness, of the sensation that feeling and action are directed from within a limited center of the organism, and that consciousness is not the mere witness of activity but the responsible agent. Yet this is something quite different from the spontaneous self-control of, say, the circulation of blood, where the control is carried out by the organism as a whole, unconsciously. For willed control brings about a sense of duality within the organism, of consciousness in conflict with appetite.

But this mode of control is a peculiar example of the proverb that nothing fails like success. For the more consciousness is individualized by the success of the will, the more everything outside the individual seems to be a threat—including not only the external world but also the "external" and uncontrolled spontaneity of one's own body, which, for example, continues to age, die, and corrupt against one's desire. Every success in control therefore demands a further success, so that the process cannot stop short of omnipotence. But this, save perhaps in some inconceivably distant future, is impossible. Hence there arises the desire to protect the ego from alien spontaneity by withdrawal from the natural world into a realm of pure consciousness or spirit.

Now withdrawal requires the inner detachment of consciousness, which is felt to be bound to nature so long as it desires it, or rather, so long as it identifies itself with the bodily organism's natural appetites. Thus it must not only control them but also cease to enjoy them. It makes little difference whether the realm of spirit be pure and formless, as in many types of mysticism, or whether it be a world of transfigured and spiritualized matter, as in Christianity. The point is that in either case will and consciousness triumph, attaining omnipotence either in their own right or by the grace of union with an omnipotent God whose whole nature is that of a self- and all-controlling will.[4]

On some such lines as these we must explain the ancient and widely prevalent conflict between spirituality and sexuality, the belief, found in East and West alike, that sexual abstinence and freedom from lust are essential prerequisites for man's proper and ultimate development. Presumably, we are free to define man's ultimate goal as we will, even if what we desire is the stimulus of eternal conflict or the repose of bodily insensitivity. But if we think of spirituality less in terms of what it avoids and more in terms of what it

[4] Yet it is curious that both nature mysticism and supernatural mysticism can arrive at experiences which are almost indistinguishable. For it would seem that the latter, in struggling not only with external nature but also with its own wayward will and desire, reaches a point of *impasse* where it discovers the perversion or selfishness of the will in the very will to struggle. It is then forced to "give itself up" to a higher power which has been conceived as the supernatural will of God. But in fact the power to which it surrenders may be the very different "omnipotence" of natural spontaneity. Thus, even when trained in a tradition of supernaturalism, the mystic may return after his experience into the world bereft of all disgust for nature. On the contrary, he is often endowed with a completely artless and childlike love for every kind of creature. In his eyes the same old world is already transfigured with the "glory of God," though to his less fortunate coreligionists it is as sinful and corrupt as ever. Cf. Dame Julian's *Revelations of the Divine Love:* "See! I am God: see! I am in all thing; see! I do all thing: see! I lift never mine hands off my works, nor ever shall, without end: see! I lead all thing to the end I ordained it to from without beginning, by the same Might, Wisdom and Love whereby I made it. How should anything be amiss?" (xi). "Sin is behovable (i.e., permissible), but all shall be well, and all shall be well, and all manner of thing shall be well" (xxvii).

is positively, and if we may think of it as including an intense awareness of the inner identity of subject and object, man and the universe, there is no reason whatsoever why it should require the rejection of sexuality. On the contrary, this most intimate of relationships of the self with another would naturally become one of the chief spheres of spiritual insight and growth.

This is in no way to say that the monastic and celibate life is an aberration, for man is not absolutely obliged to have sexual relations, nor even to eat or to live. As under certain circumstances a voluntary death or fast is perfectly justifiable, so also is sexual abstinence—in order, for example, that the force of the libido may be expended in other directions. The common mistake of the religious celibate has been to suppose that the highest spiritual life absolutely demands the renunciation of sexuality, as if the knowledge of God were an alternative to the knowledge of woman, or to any other form of experience.

Indeed, the life of total chastity is often undertaken as a monogamous marriage of the soul with God, as an all-consuming love of creature for Creator in which love for a mortal woman would be a fatal distraction. In this context sexuality is often renounced, not because it is evil, but because it is a precious and beautiful possession *offered* to God in sacrifice. But this raises the question as to whether renunciation as such is sacrifice in the proper sense of an act which "makes holy" (*sacer-facere*) the thing offered. For if sexuality is a relationship and an activity, can it be offered when neither the relationship nor the activity exists? Does a dancer offer her dancing to God by ceasing to dance? An offering can cease to exist, for its original owner, if given away to another for his use. But sacrifice is only accidentally associated with the cessation, death, or mutilation of the offering because it was once supposed that,

say, burning bulls on an altar was the only way of transport-
ing them to heaven.

The offering of sexuality to God is in all probability a survival of the idea that a woman's body, and its sexual enjoyment, is the property of her husband, to whom she is bound
to reserve herself even if he does not actually lie with her.
By analogy, the body of the celibate becomes the property
of God, dedicated to him alone. But this is not only a confusion of God with what is after all only his symbol, the
tribal father, but also the likening of the Creator-creature
relationship to a strictly barbarous conception of marriage.
Obviously, the possession of a body is not a relationship
to a person; one is related to the person only in being related to the organism of another in its total functioning.
For the human being is not a thing but a process, not an
object but a life.

The offering may be defended by saying that God uses
the sexual energy of his human spouses in other ways, diverting them into prayer or into acts of charity. With this
there can be no quarrel—provided that it does not exclude
the possibility that God may use them for sexual activity itself as an aspect of life no whit less holy than prayer or
feeding the poor. Historically, the supernaturalists have
admitted this only with great reluctance—outside the
Semitic-Islamic traditions, which have largely escaped sexual squeamishness. But the literature of the spiritual life is
overwhelmingly preoccupied with the sinful aspects of sex.
It has almost nothing to say, positively, about what holy
sex might be, save that it must be reserved to a single life
partner and consummated for the purpose of procreation
in one particular physical attitude alone!

That matrimony may be an estate as holy as virginity is
something which the Christian tradition admits theoreti-

cally, as a consequence of its Hebrew background.[5] But the force of Hebraic insistence on the goodness of things physical has had little effect on the actual feeling and practice of the Church. For from the earliest times the Church Fathers virtually equated sex with sin by identifying all sexual feeling and desire with the evil of lust. At the same time they could maintain, as against the Gnostics and Manichaeans, that the mere physical apparatus and mechanics of sex were, as God's creation, inherently pure. Speaking, then, of "ideal" sexuality as it might have been before the Fall, St. Augustine wrote:

> Those members, like the rest, would be moved by the command of his will, and the husband would be mingled with the loins of the wife without the seductive stimulus of passion, with calmness of mind and with no corruption of the innocence of the body. . . . Because the wild heat of passion would not activate those parts of the body, but, as would be proper, a voluntary control would employ them. Thus it would then have been possible to inject the semen into the womb through the female genitalia as innocently as the menstrual flow is now ejected.[6]

The general tenor and attitude of supernaturalism to sexuality is unmistakable: it is overwhelmingly negative, and to all intents and purposes the attitude is not the least modified by separating sexual mechanics from sexual feelings, a separation which in any case destroys the integrity of mind and body. Practically, if not theoretically, the basis of this attitude is the feeling that God and nature are simply

[5] Protestantism, with its greater interest in Biblical Christianity, is therefore more Hebraic in its attitude to sexuality than Catholicism, as witness Luther and Milton. But if it has to some extent liberalized sexual restraints, it has had as little notion as Catholicism of a positive sexual holiness.
[6] *De Civitate Dei*, xiv, 26.

incompatible. They may not have been so originally, but then nature was nothing like the nature we experience today. If we are to believe St. Augustine, it was something as lacking in spontaneity as artificial insemination.

Now the practical effect of a philosophy in which God and nature are incompatible is somewhat unexpected. For when the knowledge and love of God is considered to exclude other goals and other creatures, God is actually put on a par with his creatures. The knowledge of God and the knowledge of creatures can exclude one another only if they are of the same kind. One must choose between yellow and blue, as two of the kind color, but there is no need to choose between yellow and round, since what is round can also be yellow. If God is universal, the knowledge of God should include all other knowledge as the sense of sight includes all the differing objects of vision. But if the eye should attempt to see sight, it will turn in upon itself and see nothing.

Indeed, the celibate life is more appropriate to "worldly" vocations than spiritual, for while it is possible to be both a sage and a physician or artist, the exigencies of a professional or creative vocation so often suggest the Latin tag, *Aut libri aut liberi*—either books or children. But the vocation to sanctity should hardly be a specialization on the same level as writing, medicine, or mathematics, for God himself—the "object" of sanctity—is no specialist. Were he so, the universe would consist of nothing but formally religious creations—clergymen, bibles, churches, monasteries, rosaries, prayer-books, and angels.

Sanctity or sagehood as an exclusive vocation is, once again, symptomatic of an exclusive mode of consciousness in general and of the spiritual consciousness in particular. Its basic assumption is that God and nature are in competition and that man must choose between them. Its standpoint is radically dualistic, and thus it is strange indeed to find it in traditions which otherwise abjure dualism. This is a basic inconsistency, and its appearance is strangest of all in the nondualistic traditions of Indian Vedanta and Buddhism. But the confusion out of which it arises is highly instructive.

As we have seen, the relegation of sexuality and nature to the forces of evil grows out of the belief that strength and clarity of consciousness depend upon cultivating a one-pointed and exclusive mode of attention. This is, in other words, a type of attention which *ignores* the background in fastening upon the figure, and which grasps the world serially, one thing at a time. Yet this is exactly the meaning of the Hindu-Buddhist term *avidya*, ignorance, or "ignore-ance," the basic *unconsciousness* as a result of which it appears that the universe is a collection of *separate* things and events. A Buddha or "awakened one" is precisely the man who has overcome this unconsciousness and is no more bewitched by *sakaya-drishti*, the "vision of separateness." In other words, he sees each "part" of nature without ignoring its relation to the whole, without being deceived by the illusion of *māyā* which, as we also saw, is based on the idea of "measurement" (*mā-*, *mātr-*), the dividing of the world into classes, into countable things and events. So divided, the world appears to be dual (*dvaita*), but to the unobstructed vision of the sage it is in truth undivided or non-dual (*advaita*) and in this state identical with Brahman, the immeasurable and infinite reality.

Considered as a collection of separate things, the world is thus a creation of thought. *Maya*, or measuring and classifying, is an operation of the mind, and as such is the "mother" (*mata*) of a strictly abstract conception of nature, illusory in the sense that nature is so divided only in one's mind. *Maya* is illusory in an evil sense only when the

vision of the world as divided is not subordinate to the
vision of the world as undivided, when, in other words, the
cleverness of the measuring mind does not become too
much of a good thing and is "unable to see the forest for
the trees."

But the general trend of Indian thought was to fall into
the very trap which it should have avoided: it confused
the abstract world of *maya* with the concrete world of
nature, of direct experience, and then sought liberation
from nature in terms of a state of consciousness bereft of
all sense experience. It interpreted *maya* as an illusion of
the senses rather than of thought projecting itself through
the senses. In various forms of *yoga* it cultivated prolonged
exclusive concentration upon a single point—*avidya!*—in
order to exclude sense experience from consciousness, regarding it as the supreme obstacle to spiritual insight.
Above all, sense experience implied "woman," not only as a
highly attractive experience, but also as the "source" of
birth into the natural world, and thus the very incarnation
of *maya*, the Cosmic Seductress.

Thus the identification of *maya* with nature and with
woman is the classic example of deception by *maya*, of
confusing the world projected by the mind with the real
world. Yet although *maya* is figuratively the "mother" of
the projected world, projection is rather a male function
than a female. As usual, however, man projects his seed
into the woman and then accuses her of seducing him.
As Adam said, "This woman whom thou gavest me, she
tempted me and I did eat."

It was in this way that much of Indian philosophy became in practice the archetype of all world-denying dual-
isms, and in seeking liberation from sense experience became twice over the victim of *maya*. For in struggling for
release from *maya* as the concrete world of nature, it con-

firmed itself more and more deeply in the very illusion that what our minds project upon the world is what we actually see. It forgot that the senses are innocent and that self-deception is the work of thought and imagination.[7]

Confusions of this kind obscure the ways in which both sexuality and sensuality may become *maya* in its proper sense, that is, when the mind seeks more from nature than she can offer, when isolated aspects of nature are pursued in the attempt to force from them a life of joy without sorrow, or pleasure without pain. Thus the desire for sexual experience is *maya* when it is "on the brain," when it is a purely willful and imaginative craving to which the organism responds reluctantly, or not at all. Idealized and fashionable conceptions of feminine beauty are *maya* when, as is often the case, they have little relation to the actual conformations of women. Love, as de Rougemont points out, is *maya* when it is being in love with being in love, rather than a relationship with a particular woman. *Maya* is indeed Woman in the abstract.

Now sexuality is in this sense abstract whenever it is exploited or forced, when it is a deliberate, self-conscious, and yet compulsive pursuit of ecstasy, making up for the stark absence of ecstasy in all other spheres of life. Ecstasy, or transcending oneself, is the natural accompaniment of a full relationship in which we experience the "inner ᵔ- tity" between ourselves and the world. But when that re-

[7] This misinterpretation of *maya* was largely corrected in Mahayana Buddhism, especially in its Chinese form. Thus the *Lankavatara Sutra*, ii, 18, states that nirvana or release from *maya* is not to be understood as "the future annihilation of the senses and their fields." So, too, the Chinese Zen master Seng-ts'an says explicitly:

> Do not be antagonistic to the world of the senses,
> For when you are not antagonistic to it,
> It turns out to be the same as complete Awakening.

Likewise Kuo-an in his comments upon the *Ten Oxherding Pictures* says, "Things oppress us not because of an objective world, but because of a self-deceiving mind."

lationship is hidden and the individual feels himself to be a restricted island of consciousness, his emotional experience is largely one of restriction, and it is as arid as the abstract *persona* which he believes himself to be. But the sexual act remains the one easy outlet from his predicament, the one brief interval in which he transcends himself and yields consciously to the spontaneity of his organism. More and more, then, this act is expected to compensate for defective spontaneity in all other directions, and is therefore abstracted or set apart from other experiences as *the* great delight.

Such abstract sexuality is thus the certain result of a forced and studied style of personality, and of confusing spirituality with mere will power—a confusion which remains even when one is *willing* one's will over to God. The individual ascetic may indeed succeed in sublimating his desire for sexual ecstasy into some other form, but he remains part of a society, a culture, upon which his attitude to sex has a powerful influence. By associating sex with evil he makes *the* great delight an even greater fascination for the other members of his society, and thereby unknowingly assists the growth of all the refinements of civilized lust. Considered from the standpoint of society as a whole, puritanism is as much a method of exploiting sex by titillation as black underwear, since it promotes the same shocking and exciting contrast between the naked flesh and the black of clerical propriety. It would not be unreasonable to regard puritanism, like masochism, as an extreme form of sexual "decadence."

The culture of Victorian England offers a striking example of this religious prurience, since it was by no means so sexless and staid as has often been supposed, but was, on the contrary, a culture of the most elegant lasciviousness. Extreme modesty and prudishness in the home so heightened the fascination of sex that prostitution, even for the upper classes, flourished on a far greater scale than in our own relatively liberal times. Fashionable and respectable boarding schools combined a total repression of overt sexuality with a proportionably flagrant indulgence in flagellomania. Fashions in clothing did everything to reveal and accentuate the feminine outline in the very act of covering it from neck to toe in veritable strait jackets of tweed, flannel, and boned corsetry. Even the chairs, tables, and household ornaments were suggestively bulged and curved—the chairs wide-shouldered and then waisted at the back, the seat broad, and the legs so obviously thighs or calves that squeamish housewives made the resemblance all the stronger by fitting them with skirts. For when sexuality is repressed in its direct manifestation, it irradiates other spheres of life to scatter on every side symbols and suggestions of its all the more urgent presence.

From the standpoint of cultural anthropology this back-handed manner of embellishing sexuality may be just one of many legitimate variants of the art of sex. For so sensitive a creature as man, art is natural. He does not care to masticate raw beef with hands and teeth, nor to make love with the same "natural" unconcern as that with which he sneezes, nor to live in homes thrown together anyhow to keep out the wet and cold. Therefore there is almost always an art of love, whether it be as directly concerned with the sexual act as the Indian *Kamasutra*, or a preoccupation with the long preliminaries of wooing to which the sexual act itself is merely the final swift climax. Puritanism is simply one of these variants—that is, if we look at it as a natural phenomenon and do not take it at its own valuation of itself. It is another case of serving nature in trying to work against her, of an extreme of human artifice being no less natural than the supposedly freakish creatures of the wild. It is simply damming a stream to increase its force, but doing so unintentionally or unconsciously. Thus it has often been noted that periods of license and periods of puritanism alternate, the latter creating an excitement that can no longer be contained, and the former a lassitude that requires reinvigoration. The more normal means of keeping the stream at an even strength is modesty rather than prudery, the heightening of sexual fascination by aesthetic concealment as distinct from moral condemnation.[8]

But if puritanism and cultivated licentiousness are not fundamental deviations from nature, they are simply the opposite poles of one and the same attitude—that, right or wrong, sexual pleasure is *the* great delight.[9] This attitude, like the cultivation of the ego, is indeed one of the innumerable possibilities of the freedom of our nature, but because it abstracts sexuality from the rest of life (or *attempts* to do so), it hardly begins to realize its possibilities. Abstract sexuality is partial—a function of dissociated brains instead of total organisms—and for this reason is a singular confusion of the natural world with the *maya* of intellectual divisions and categories. For when sexuality is set apart as

[8] Thus the Chinese and Japanese, who do not suffer from sexual guilt, have a strong sense of sexual shame, and have difficulty in appreciating our ready representation of the nude in art. Writing from Europe in 1900, a mandarin said, "The pictures in the palace set apart for them would not please the cultured mind of my venerable brother. The female form is represented nude or half nude. This would obtain fault from our propriety. . . . They have statues of plaster, and some of marble, in the public gardens and in this palace, most of them naked. In the winter's ice it makes me want to cover them. The artists do not know the attraction of rich flowing drapery." Hwuy-ung, *A Chinaman's Opinion of Us and His Own Country*. London, 1927.
[9] Thus a recent summary of the compendia of Catholic moral theology, Jone's *Moral Theology* (Newman Press, 1952), devotes 44 pages to a discussion of the various categories of sin, of which 32, in fine print, are occupied with sexual sins—showing their relative importance with respect to murder, greed, cruelty, lying, and self-righteousness.

a specially good or specially evil compartment of life, it no longer works in full relation to everything else. In other words, it loses universality. It becomes a part doing duty for the whole—the idolatry of a creature worshipped in place of God, and an idolatry committed as much by the ascetic as the libertine.

So long, then, as sexuality remains this abstract *maya* it remains a "demonic" and unspiritualized force, unspiritual in the sense that it is divorced from the universal and concrete reality of nature. For we are trying to wrest it from subordination to the total pattern of organism-environment relationship which, in Chinese philosophy, is *li*—the ordering principle of the Tao. But the universalization of sex involves far more than Freud's recognition that art, religion, and politics are expressions of sublimated libido. We must also see that sexual relations are religious, social, metaphysical, and artistic. Thus the "sexual problem" cannot be solved simply at the sexual level, for which reason our whole discussion makes it subordinate to the problem of man and nature. Sexuality will remain a problem so long as it continues to be the isolated area in which the individual transcends himself and experiences spontaneity. He must first allow himself to be spontaneous in the whole play of inner feeling and of sensory response to the everyday world. Only as the senses in general can learn to accept without grasping, or to be conscious without straining, can the special sensations of sex be free from the grasping of abstract lust and its inseparable twin, the inhibition of abstract or "spiritual" disgust.

It is in this way alone that the problem can be taken out of the fruitlessly alternating dualism in which we have set it. In this dualism sexuality is now good and now bad, now lustful and now prudish, now compellingly grasped and now guiltily inhibited. For when sexual activity is sought in the abstract its disappointments are proportionate to its exaggerated expectations, associating themselves with the swift transition from extreme excitement to lassitude which accompanies detumescence. The aftermath of intercourse, which should be a state of fulfilled tranquillity, is for the prude the depression of guilt and for the libertine the depression of ennui. The reason is that both are grasping at the sensation of intense lust which immediately precedes the orgasm, making it a goal rather than a gift, and so experienced it is an elation which swings over to depression, its opposite *maya*. But when the mounting excitement is accepted rather than grasped, it becomes a full realization of spontaneity, and the resulting orgasm is not its sudden end but the bursting in upon us of peace.

It will by now be clear that a truly natural sexuality is by no means a spontaneity in the sense of promiscuity breaking loose from restraint. No more is it the colorlessly "healthy" sexuality of mere animal release from biological tension. To the degree that we do not yet know what man is, we do not yet know what human sexuality is. We do not know what man is so long as we know him piecemeal, categorically, as the separate individual, the agglomeration of blocklike instincts and passions and sensations regarded one by one under the fixed stare of an exclusive consciousness. What man is, and what human sexuality is, will come to be known only as we lay ourselves open to experience with the full sensitivity of feeling which does not grasp.

The experience of sexual love is therefore no longer to be sought as the repetition of a familiar ecstasy, prejudiced by the expectation of what we already know. It will be the exploration of our relationship with an ever-changing, ever unknown partner, unknown because he or she is not in truth the abstract role or person, the set of conditioned reflexes which society has imposed, the stereotyped male or female which education has led us to expect. All these are *maya*, and the love of these is the endlessly frustrating love of fantasy. What is not *maya* is mystery, what cannot be described or measured, and it is in this sense—symbolized by the veil of modesty—that woman is always a mystery to man, and man to woman. It is in this sense that we must understand van der Leeuw's remarkable saying that "the mystery of life is not a problem to be solved, but a reality to be experienced."

7: Sacred and Profane Love

IT IS ALWAYS INSTRUCTIVE TO GO BACK TO
the original meanings of words to discover not only what
new senses they have gained, but also what old senses they
have lost. The word "profane," for example, did not at first
signify the blasphemous or irreligious, but an area or court
before (*pro*) the entrance to a temple (*fanum*). It was thus
the proper place of worship for the common people as
distinct from the initiates, though here again the "common"
is not the crude but the communal—the people living in
society. By contrast, the sacred was not the merely religious but what lay outside or beyond the community, what
was—again in an ancient sense—*extraordinary* or outside
the social order.

But we seem to have lost sight of the fact that there can
be a position outside the communal and conventional order
which is not subversive, a position free from rule but not
against it. Almost invariably we confuse this position with
its opposite—that which lies below order, and which is
chaos rather than freedom. It is part of the same confusion
that speaking with "authority" has come to mean speaking
for the government, the Church, or tradition, or with the
backing of well-documented footnotes. Yet it was not thus
that Jesus was described as "speaking as one having authority, and not as the Scribes." The point was that he
spoke with inner conviction, which must again be distinguished from the dogmatism of inner uncertainty. The
"original" has likewise come to mean the novel or even ec-

centric, but the deeper senses of authority and originality are to be the author and origin of one's own deeds as a free agent. The socially conditioned *persona* or role-playing ego is, however, never a free agent. Man is free to the extent that he realizes his genuine self to be the author and origin of nature.

Yet here again our accustomed confusion of levels makes this indistinguishable from the lunatic boast "I myself am God!" Out of this confusion the Western Church rejected the insight of Eckhart in saying:

> God must be very I, I very God, so consummately one that this he and this I are one "is," in this is-ness working one work eternally; but so long as this he and this I, to wit, God and the soul, are not one single here, one single now, the I cannot work with nor be one with that he.[1]

For the root of the confusion is that the Christian tradition of the West has lacked what we have called "inwardness." Its official position has always been profane, conventional, and exoteric without knowing it to be so. Thus it has confused the profane with the sacred, the relative with the absolute, the social sphere of law and order with the divine nature. The social order has therefore been enforced with sanctions which are too strong, and its laws have been made absolute imperatives. We have already seen this in the notion that the love of God and the love of nature can be considered alternatives, like mutually exclusive creatures and things. But when God, the Absolute, is thus dragged down into the realm of creatures and made to compete with them, the order of creatures, of society and convention, is blasted. For when the ear is singing, all other sounds are lost.

This is why Christian officialdom is itself the cause of

[1] Tr. Evans (1), vol. 1, p. 247.

the very secularism and shallow relativism which it so much condemns. For the secular revolution of the Renaissance and the Enlightenment and all that followed was a parody of the "mystery" which the Church had neglected. This was the strictly inner or sacred doctrine that in God, in reality, all men are free and equal, or, to put it in another way, that in God there are no classes or distinctions, no respect of persons. For the initiate into this mystery has

> put on the new man, which is renewed in knowledge after the image of him that created him: where there is neither Greek nor Jew, circumcision nor uncircumcision, Barbarian, Scythian, bond nor free; but Christ is all, and in all.[2]

A state Church, which is to say a profane Church, could not possibly admit or cherish such a doctrine, and thus when it was dragged out of neglect it became a pretext for revolution, and the Church could not claim it, saying, "Come, this is nothing new. We have known it all the time and are now ready to explain it to you correctly."

Instead, the Church virtually disowned its inner meaning, retreated into an ever more rigid identification of God with law, and abandoned the position beyond good and evil and beyond distinctions to the secularists. But here it became the position *below* good and evil. Standards were not transcended but rejected, and equality in the sight of God became the assumption that all men are equally inferior. Freedom became mere individualism, and the classless society a dull uniformity. Art became monotonous eccentricity, and craft monotonous mass production. These are sweeping generalizations to which there have been happy exceptions, but the consistent trend of the so-called modern or progressive spirit has been toward an obliteration of social distinctions which is, in effect, a dis-

[2] Colossians 3, 10–11.

organization of society. For the organic is always differen-
tiated, in function if not in worth.

One of the most extreme forms of this parody is the attitude of so many Freudians which reduces all creative
activity—art, philosophy, religion, and literature—to a
manifestation of oral or anal eroticism, or infantile in-
cestuousness, with the cynical implication that all men are
thereby equally guilty. The transparent feeling of this attitude is not that these libidinous foundations are natural
and pure, but that poets and sages can be debunked by
being reduced to a level which, to these psychologists
themselves, is still obscene. This resembles nothing so
much as the "police psychology" which assumes that all
men, the policemen included, are criminals and holds it
over their heads. In such instances it comes out very clearly
that this parody of the doctrine of equality is the tragic
and destructive resentment of creativity by the under-
privileged or unloved.

These are not, however, the people of *low* status: they
are the people of *no* status, bred in profusion by a society
which confuses the moral law with the divine nature. For
such a society cannot give any status to what is low—to
the gambler, courtesan, drunkard, beggar, sexual deviant,
or tramp. In a system of absolutist morals such people have
no place at all. They are unacceptable to God since there
are no longer allowed to be any *least* in the Kingdom of
Heaven, and his sun may no longer shine upon the unjust
unless they consent to reform. But the unjust are not only
special classes of people; unjust or unadjusted elements
exist in every member of society as the ignored aspects of
nature which do not fit in with *maya*, the conventional order. They are, in a technical sense, obscene or "off-scene" [3]

[3] On second thought I forget the source of the article in which I came
across this suggestive but probably dubious derivation of the word. Ac-

because they do not come into the picture; they have no outward role or part in the social drama. Nevertheless, they are as essential to it as the stagehands behind the scenes, the faces behind the masks, and the bodies beneath the costumes.

But when the conventional order and the divine nature are confused, the unjust and the obscene become metaphysically sinful—absolutely intolerable to God. And what is intolerable to God becomes, in another way, intolerable to man. He cannot support a situation in which the ignored and obscene parts of his nature are brought out onto the stage and condemned. His only defense is to accuse the accusers, to unmask and unfrock everyone, saying, "Look, you are *really* just like me!" Yet this in its own way is just as much a mistake as the confusion which provoked it. The off-scene is not the *reality* behind the outward drama: it is also part of the illusion, for what is to be off-scene is determined by the selection of what is to be on-scene; what is ignored is relative to what is noticed. Herein is the error of supposing that repressed sexual forces are the realities behind cultural achievements, for the relationship between them is one of mutuality and not of subordination. While the evil is defined by the choice of the good, it is not the reality determining the choice.

Thus when the sacred idea of equality is profaned it turns out to be the parody that in reality, in God, all men are alike in their obscenity. What it should have meant

cording to the Oxford English Dictionary the etymology of "obscene" is unknown, whereas Webster derives it from *obs-caenum*, with *caenum* meaning "filth," though such a combination would ordinarily have appeared in English as "occene." However, the sense of "off-scene" is consistent with an alternative derivation from *ob-scaenum* (Greek, σκαιός), designating the left-hand, sinister, and inauspicious. For both the off-scene and the sinister have to do with the indispensable underside or dark aspect of things. Inauspicious as it may be, the left must always accompany the right.

is that in reality all men are alike in their essential inno-
cence—that the division of their natures into the good and
the evil, the on-scene and off-scene, is (in another original
sense of a word) *arbitrary* or a decision of an independent
spectator, none other than our old friend the isolated, observing ego. But to the eye of God there is no distinction
of on-scene and off-scene, and all men are just as they are,
as the Buddhists would say, of "one suchness." When the
curtain falls and all the actors come out in front with the
author and the director *as themselves* and no longer in
their roles, the hero and the villain, the men on-scene and
the men off-scene are alike applauded.

Therefore judge nothing before the time, until the Lord
come, who both will bring to light the hidden things of
darkness, and will make manifest the counsels of the hearts:
and then shall every man have praise of God.[4]

At times, however, the audience will be moved to boo.
But they will not boo the villain because he *was* the villain;
they will boo him, at the end of the play, if he did not act
true to character. They will boo if what should have stayed
off-scene has kept coming on-scene, or *vice versa*. In other
words, there is nothing wrong with the obscene so long as it

---

[4] 1 Corinthians 4, 5. St. Paul is often so quotable in senses that are
probably out of context and which would doubtless have horrified him.
However, I would like to see someone make a case for the idea that the
Apostles really did hand down an inner tradition to the Church, and that
through all these centuries the Church has managed to guard it from the
public eye. If so, it has remained far more secret and "esoteric" than in
any of the other great spiritual traditions of the world, so much so that
its existence is highly doubtful. For in the West the *philosophia perennis*
has always been an individual matter, often condemned and sometimes
barely tolerated by the official hierarchy. It would, however, be much
easier to make a case of this kind for the Eastern Orthodox Church than
for the Roman Catholic. On the other hand, a true esotericism is not a
matter of "secret information," formally withheld from public knowledge.
It is secret in the sense of ineffable, that is, a mode of knowledge which
cannot be described because it does not fall into any class.

remains off the scene and stays in its place. But in a moral absolutism it *has* no place—perhaps because the audience does not know that the play is a play. The social drama and its conventions are confused with reality.

The proper distinction of the sacred from the profane, and of the profane from the obscene, is of the utmost importance for a philosophy of love as between man and woman. Failure to see the difference between the sacred and the profane is one of the main reasons why the Christian tradition has no adequate idea of sacred love. For sacred love is not the love of God as an alternative to the love of creatures. Sacred love is not matrimony, though it may sometimes exist between the married. Nor is sacred love the "grand passion" in its popular and romantic sense. Just as we have a parody of equality before God in modern secularism, we have also a parody of sacred love which has arisen in much the same way.

It is common knowledge that the institution of marriage came to the West as a highly formal familial arrangement, a character which in some Latin countries it still retains. The founding of the branch of a family was by no means a matter of private choice, but a momentous decision involving many people. It was therefore arranged, not by the young couple, but by grandfathers and grandmothers, and stabilized by legal contracts which the modern version of the institution still involves. Whether the couple "loved" each other, or might come to do so, was a thing of minor importance. The marriage represented a familial alliance, and was governed by political, social, and—however "primitive"—eugenic considerations. In cultures where this form of marriage still exists, concubinage and other forms of extramarital sexuality flourish as a matter of course *for men*, even when tolerated rather than provided for by law. In general, such extramarital relations are off-scene, existing by a social agreement which is tacit but not explicit. Marriage was therefore a profane institution—a matter of communal convention as between people who were playing social roles. Therefore those who were above role, or, as in India, above caste, did not marry or at least abandoned marriage when the time came for their liberation from *maya*.

Now, Christianity arose in the West as an exceedingly strange mixture of social and religious ideas from many different sources. It comprised legal and social ideas of marriage that were mainly Jewish with notions of moral and spiritual chastity that were Greek or Essene, and probably garbled and remote influences from India. The resulting confusion was so involved that it may assist us to unravel it if we simply list the main factors that came into play:

1. The Jewish idea that the physical universe is inherently good.
2. The Orphic and garbled Indian idea that the physical universe is evil.
3. The Jewish institution of marriage as a property and familial arrangement.
4. The Jewish idea of the holiness of procreation, the duty of population increase, and the sin of sowing the human seed unprocreatively.
5. The Orphic-Essene-Indian idea of withdrawal from the flesh through nonprocreation, and thus of the greater holiness of virginity.
6. The Jewish idea of the sin of adultery as an infringement of property rights.
7. The generally Greco-Indian tradition that the holy or sacred person stands apart from social involvement.
8. The Jewish idea that the social conventions are the laws of God.

9. Jesus' own idea that women, too, have some rights since
   they are at least equal with men in having souls.

It is no wonder that an attempt to combine these ideas
plunged the relations between men and women into a
fearsome mess, though it may perhaps have been worth
while if only for the last idea involved—the recognition
that "women are people."

But to appreciate the full extent of the confusion we
must consider the fact that Indian ideas had reached the
West in an extremely popularized and literal form, a form
which they had of course assumed in India itself in the first
place. The main feature of this distortion was the confusion
of *maya* with evil on the one hand and with the natural
universe on the other. This involved the further confusion
of the virgin or sacred person with the totally abstinent,
the person withdrawn not only from society but also from
nature. But the original meaning of a *parthenos* or virgin
was a woman who did not submit to arranged marriage,
taking, instead, a partner of her own choice. She became
an "unmarried mother" not because she was vicious or
promiscuous, but because she was a person in her own
right.

Now the early Church combined all these diverse factors
by preserving the legal, familial marriage, restricting it to
one wife, and virtually outlawing divorce out of respect for
women's rights. Consistently, the next step would have
been to extend the tacit recognition of off-scene sexuality
to women, but instead it merely forbade it to men. Jesus
attacked divorce because a divorced woman was like mer-
chandise returned to the seller as unfit for use, as a result
of which she lost social status altogether. The important
point, however, was that the type of marriage which the
Church monogamized and protected against divorce, and

from which it excluded concubinage, was the familial *arranged* marriage.[5] Sexual love in any other sense than illicit and sinful lust is a matter which the New Testament totally ignores.[6]

In short, the Church combined the Jewish insistence on procreation and the Greco-Indian ideal of sexual abstinence in a form of marriage which would effect the greatest possible restriction of sexual feeling. In this way the profane institution of marriage was identified, or rather confused, with the sacred state of chastity, which was in turn mistaken for joyless sexuality or, preferably, abstinent virginity. As St. Paul said, "Let those with wives be as though they had none." The outcome, the sacrament of Holy Matrimony, was supposed to be the sanctification of the profane by the sacred by analogy with the union of the Word with the flesh in the Incarnation. But because

[5] "The girl is not consulted about her espousals, for she awaits the judgment of her parents, inasmuch as a girl's modesty will not allow her to choose a husband." St. Ambrose, *De Abraham*, i, *ad fin*. St. Basil, *Ep. ad Amphilocium*, ii, says that a marriage without paternal sanction is fornication, and under the laws of Constantius and Constans it was a capital offense.

[6] However, the celebrated text of Matthew 5, 28, imputing adultery to so much as looking on a woman to lust after her should be taken in context. The whole passage from verse 17 to the end is an ironical discussion of the legal righteousness of the Pharisees. Jesus shows the shallowness and absurdity of legal righteousness by taking it to an extreme. He begins with what to any but the most simple-minded literalist would be the obvious jest that the very punctuation marks and calligraphic ornaments of the law are now to be sacrosanct. He then arranges various types of anger and abuse in descending order of gravity, but assigns penalties for them in the reverse order. For unreasonable anger, the magistrate's court is assigned; for saying "Raca" or "silly idiot," the high court; and for saying "You fool," hellfire itself. But in Matthew 23, 17, Jesus uses the selfsame expression, "You fools" ($\mu\omega\rho o i$), in speaking to the followers of the Pharisees. In the verse in question he satirizes the property law against adultery by extending it to a similar extreme, and then goes on to recommend the excision of the lustful eye. The passage can be taken at its face value only on the assumption that Jesus was totally lacking in humor.

the Word and the Spirit, as conceived, were really anti-
thetical to the flesh, and the sacred *opposed* to the profane, the coming together of the two was not a union but
an enslavement. Similarly, as the male stood for the spirit
and the female for the flesh, the wife had no choice of her
partner and must be subservient to her husband.

This was obviously a conception of marriage which could
not last, but it was some time before it was modified by the
exercise of mutual choice by the two partners. As the
Church became identified with the state and as its early
zeal flagged, Holy Matrimony was in practice modified in
many ways, mainly through reversion to polygyny, concubinage, and prostitution.[7] But the factor which transformed the Christian conception of marriage more than
anything else was the emergence in the early Middle Ages
of the cult of courtly love, which is the historical basis of
what we now know as the romantic conception of love and
marriage.

Historians are not in clear agreement as to the origins
and nature of this extraordinary movement, but the weight
of opinion is that the Catharist heresy, from which it arose,
was a form of the Persian religion of Manichaeism, of
which vestiges remained in Western Europe from the
days of the Roman Empire, or which was reintroduced by
returning crusaders. Now, Manichaeism was a syncretist
movement and seems to have been one of the principal car-
riers of distorted Indian ideas to the West. These included
an extreme dualism of spirit and nature reminiscent of the
Samkhya philosophy, and a conception of love as "pure desire" which is strangely similar to forms of the Indian cult
of Tantra, in which the arousal and transmutation of sexual desire was employed as a type of yoga. The spiritual
ideal of Manichaeism was the liberation of the world of

[7] G. R. Taylor (1), pp. 19–50.

light from the world of darkness, and thus the deliverance of the human spirit from its fleshly prison.

The conception of "pure desire" as well as the dualist distortion of the *maya* doctrine had, indeed, reached the West before the appearance of Catharism, for we find St. John Chrysostom, St. Gregory of Nazianzus, and St. Jerome condemning the spread among Christians of taking to themselves *agapetae* or *virgines subintroductae*. This was the practice of forming a love relationship with virgin Christian girls which went as far as caressing and sleeping with them, and perhaps involved *coitus reservatus,* but avoided actual emission of the seed. By this means sexual desire was not "dissipated" in orgasm but was restrained and built up into passion. To put it in another way, its restraint at the sexual center caused it to irradiate the whole organism, transmuting the atmosphere of sexual feeling into every phase of the relationship between the partners. In such a way sexual attraction was personalized. It became a desire not just for "woman," but for the particular woman whose whole body and whose day-to-day associations with her lover had become "perfumed" with restrained and irradiated lust. In this way, too, the beloved became idealized; she became more than mere woman; she became a goddess, image of the divine.

Repressed for a time by the official Church, the practice appeared again in Europe in the twelfth century, now in the form of Catharism and courtly love. But here the women involved were not only or chiefly virgins, but married women, often the wives of feudal princes, with whom young knights formed the bond of *donnoi.* This was apparently an "ideal" or "sexually pure" love relationship wherein sexual feeling was transmuted into all the attentions and gallantries which became expected of a *gentleman* toward a lady. These relationships formed the themes

of troubadour poetry, the chief wellspring of all later Euro-
pean secular poetry, as well as the entire basis of the Western notion of ideal or romantic love.

Historians disagree as to whether these relationships
were genuinely "ideal" or simply a cloak for refined adultery and fornication, the latter impression being founded
on the many references in the poetic literature to caressing
and embracing the naked body of the beloved lady. At
the same time, there are equally frequent references to
the absolute necessity of avoiding actual sexual intercourse, for as one of the poets said, "He knows nothing of
donnoi who wants fully to possess his lady." Although,
then, there is no direct evidence for the fact, the very am-
biguity of the references suggests that the relationship
often extended to *coitus reservatus* or, to use the Persian
word, *karezza*—the prolonged sexual union without orgasm on the part of the male.

But whether *karezza* was employed or not, it is clear that
courtly love introduced a contemplative as distinct from
an active mode of sexuality—a distinction parallel to the
religious differentiation between the contemplative and
active lives. For the ideal of the troubadour was at least
to gaze upon and worship the unveiled form of his lady.
In this respect the troubadours had grasped one of the
elements of sacred love, that is, of a love relationship consistent with and patterned after the contemplative life. It
is important to remember that the contemplative life is
not to be confused with the merely cloistered life, which,
however, sometimes includes it. Essentially the contemplative life is the summit of spiritual insight—the vision
or *theoria* of God—a realization permeating all one's ordinary and practical activities. In just the same way, the
troubadour wished to contemplate his lady and have his
whole life permeated by the atmosphere of her presence.

Although courtly love was adopted by individual members of the clergy and the *donnoi* relationship was often blessed with ecclesiastical rites, the cult was in the end subject to the most ruthless persecution which the Church has ever sponsored, prior to the Reformation. The Dominican campaign against the Cathars or Albigenses involved also an attempt to substitute the Virgin Mary for the idealized woman of courtly devotion. But the persecution never eradicated the process which changed Christian matrimony into the ideal of a fulfillment of romantic love—an ideal which, in later times, the Church itself adopted. Thus modern Catholic theories of Christian marriage differ so radically from the conceptions of the Patristic age just because they have absorbed so much from the philosophy of courtly love. This, rather than the few hints of the idea in the Gospels and St. Paul, is the real root of the modern Christian doctrine of married love. Few modern Catholic theologians regard matrimony as the mere restriction of sexual relations to one woman for the purpose of procreating Christian children. The emphasis has now passed to the idea of loving a woman as a person, as *this* woman rather than "woman," for in such a way marital love becomes analogous to God's own love, conceived as his eternal faithfulness to each and every individual person.

There is no doubt that this modern view of Holy Matrimony is a tremendous improvement upon what was originally nothing more than a rigid restriction of the arranged marriage and a total condemnation of sexual feeling. But it is still a parody of sacred love, and arises from the Church's inability to distinguish the profane from the sacred by making the two mutually exclusive, which is to say, of the same kind.[8]

[8] There are other instructive examples of the confusion. Thus the term "person," originally the *per-sona* or megaphone-mask indicating the as-

One of the best apologists for the modern ideal of Holy Matrimony is the Catholic-minded Protestant Denis de Rougemont, whose important work *Love in the Western World* is at the same time a marvellous clarification and a profound misunderstanding of the differences between sacred and profane love. The gist of his thesis is that mature sexual love is total devotion to the entirety of another human being—as distinct from bodily lust or passion, which he describes as being in love with being in love, passion in particular being an infatuation with the subjective feelings aroused by postponing sexual intercourse with an idealized woman. But he is surely mistaken in thinking that passion, as cultivated by the troubadours, stands alongside pure eroticism or "pagan love" in opposition to his own ideal of matrimony. For he sees both of the former as an attitude to woman in which she is merely the pretext for an ecstasy, whether it be self-frustrating passion or self-indulging lust. Yet the problem is not so simple, for it is precisely from courtly love that modern Christianity has obtained the idea that, in Holy Matrimony, sexual love may be completely fused with personal love.

We must repeat that in its early centuries Christianity had no conception of the hallowing of sexual feeling. Sexual intercourse between a married couple was pure to the

sumed role of the player in classical drama, is used to designate the basic spiritual reality of the human being and God alike. The human being is said to have spiritual dignity because he is a person, as God is three Persons. But a person is strictly what one is as a mask or role, at the social and conventional level. The word which should have been used for the ego is used for the self (*atman*) or spirit (*pneuma*), which in other traditions is supra-individual. Hence the Christian identification of the spirit with the ego, and the inability to see that man is more than ego, that his true and basic selfhood is divine. Another instance appears in the celibacy of the *secular* priesthood, indicating a confusion of the sacerdotal *caste* (profane) with the casteless (sacred) contemplatives —the monks and hermits who have abandoned worldly (or social) estate (or class). As we have seen, matters are made worse by the confusion of abandoning estate or status with abandoning nature.

extent that it was a brief physical exchange for procreation. The wife was loved and cherished inasmuch as, having an immortal soul, she was, after all, as good as another *man*. To lust after one's wife was little short of adultery. It was, then, from Manichaeans and Cathars that Christians learned the art of personalizing sexual desire, that is, of delaying the haste of lust so that sexual feeling would attach itself not merely to the subpersonal organs and limbs of the woman but to her total personality. The modern view of Holy Matrimony is therefore a middle position between the early Christian and the courtly, allowing sufficient passion, or delay of lust, to personalize the relationship and, unlike the Cathars, permitting the male orgasm so as to produce children and to prevent passion from becoming an end in itself. But the historical roots of this view are not purely Christian.

Even so, this conception of matrimony is far short of realizing what the sexual relationship may be at the sacred level. This is evident in the fact that de Rougemont identifies the sacred element in matrimony with fidelity to the legal or profane contract between the partners. As he sees it, the whole dignity and responsibility of being a person is realized in strength of will—in being able to stand by one's *word*, in the irrevocable decision of the couple to make their contractual pledge stand firm against all nonverbal, natural, fleshly, or emotional considerations. This is, he confesses, an absurdity against all practical reason, but such is precisely the divine absurdity of Christianity, of which Tertullian said, *Credo quia absurdum est*— "I believe because it is absurd."

Forgoing any rationalist or hedonist form of apology, I propose to speak only of a troth that is observed *by virtue of the absurd*—that is to say, simply because it has been pledged—and by virtue of being an absolute which will up-

hold the husband and wife as persons. . . . I maintain that
fidelity thus understood is the best means we have of becoming persons. The person is manifested in the making. What
is person within each of us is an entity built up like a work
of art—built up thanks to constructiveness and in the same
conditions as we construct things. . . . Neither passion nor
the heretical faith out of which it sprang could have inspired
the belief that the control of Nature should be the aim of
our lives.[9]

Here in a nutshell is the whole story of the identification of the absolute, the personal, and the divine with
artifice in opposition to nature. In its original meaning the
persona, the mask, is indeed a construct, a *maya* in its
proper sense. But for this very reason it should have been
distinguished from the divine and the absolute. For the
divine, the real, is not the construct; it is the natural, nonverbal, and indescribable order (*li*) from which construction emerges and to which it is subordinate. To set the
principle of artifice and construction outside and against
nature is to tear the universe apart in such a way that the
rift can only be healed upon the terms of the total submis-
sion of nature to the will and its legal violence. Such a view
of the divinity of the law and the word issues in a conception of the marriage contract where man is made for
the Sabbath, not the Sabbath for man. For man is held to
acquire personality or spiritual dignity by submitting himself irrevocably to an absolute law. Faithfulness is thereby
confused with complete mistrust of oneself, for on these
terms the human organism is to be trusted only in so far as
it binds itself to a law—a law which it has itself invented,
and whose order and structure is far inferior to his own.

It was for this reason that Confucius made *jen* or "human-

[9] De Rougemont (1), pp. 307–8.

heartedness" a far higher virtue than *i* or "righteousness," and declined to give the former any clear definition. For man cannot define or legalize his own nature. He may attempt to do so only at the cost of identifying himself with an abstract and incomplete image of himself—that is, with a mechanical principle which is qualitatively inferior to a man. Thus Confucius felt that in the long run human passions and feelings were more trustworthy than human principles of right and wrong, that the natural man was more of a man than the conceptual man, the constructed person. Principles were excellent, and indeed necessary, so long as they were tempered with human-heartedness and the sense of proportion or humor that goes with it. War, for example, is less destructive when fought for greed than for the justification of ideological principles, since greed will not destroy what it wishes to possess, whereas the vindication of principle is an abstract goal which is perfectly ruthless in regard to the humane values of life, limb, and property.

Zealots and fanatics of all kinds revolt at Confucian reasonableness, with its spirit of compromise and mellow humor, feeling it to be ignoble and tame, lacking the heroism and fire of irrevocable commitment to principle—and this is precisely the attitude of Chinese Communism in its present attempt to destroy the Confucian tradition.[10] But from the Confucian standpoint the zealotry of irrevocable commitment to principle is not only a silly bravado and a striking of heroic attitudes; it is also a total insensitivity to inner feeling and to the subtle intelligence of the natural order. "The superior man," said Confucius in the *Analects*, "goes through life without any one preconceived course of

[10] See Arthur F. Wright, "Struggle *versus* Harmony: Symbols of Competing Values in Modern China," in Bryson, *et al.*, *Symbols and Values*, pp. 589-602. Harper, New York, 1954.

action or any taboo. He merely decides for the moment what is the right thing to do." [11]

From our standpoint such a precept is the recommendation of caprice and disorder, for we feel that unless the artifice of law is held over our heads like a club we shall revert to our "basic" and "natural" depravity, as if this is what we really are under the "veneer" of civilization. This is not, however, what we are really, naturally, and basically. It is what we are off-scene, which, as we saw, is no more real than what we are on-scene. Unseemly disorderliness is, in fact, the last thing of which anyone would accuse followers of the Confucian and Taoist philosophies, since they have formed the foundations of one of the most stable societies in the world.

It will now be clear that we must discover the character of sacred love by analogy with the sacred or contemplative life in its other aspects. But it had first to be clear that the sacred is not in competition with the profane as if it were something of the same kind. In other words, the sacred is not in the conceptual and conventional order of things, and thus neither fights with them, avoids them, nor struggles to dominate them. It has no need to do so, for it is the superior order out of which they proceed and to which they are always eventually subordinate—and this is why every attempted escape from sexuality transforms itself into prurience. "Tao is that from which one cannot for a single instant depart. That from which one may depart is not Tao." [12]

In the life of spontaneity human consciousness shifts from the attitude of strained, willful attention to *kuan*, the attitude of open attention or contemplation. This at-

---

[11] Cf. de Rougemont (1), p. 308: "The pledge exchanged in marriage is the very type of a *serious* act, because it is a pledge given once and for all. The irrevocable alone is serious!"

[12] *Chung-yung, i.*

titude forms the basis of a more "feminine" and receptive approach to love, an attitude which for that very reason is more considerate of women. It will have been obvious that most of the attitudes hitherto discussed are one-sidedly and ridiculously male. Save among the practitioners of *karezza*, they know nothing of the female orgasm, which, for purposes of simple procreation, is almost irrelevant. They are thus exclusively concerned with the rights and wrongs of male pleasure in sex, and, furthermore, of a male approach which is one-sidedly aggressive, domineering, and grasping. In short, they are attempts to make rules for sexuality by people who knew extremely little about it.

The idea of equality in the sacred sphere has often been taken to mean the disappearance of sexuality, since St. Paul said that in Christ there is neither male nor female, and Jesus said that in heaven there is neither marriage nor giving in marriage. But the latter remark is only to say that heaven, the sacred sphere, stands above the social institutions of the profane sphere. Conversely, the secular notion of sexual equality is one that merely permits women to behave like men, and the two parodies, the Churchly and the secular, are equally sexless rather than sexually equal. Sexual equality should properly mean sexual fulfillment, the woman realizing her masculinity through man, and the man realizing his femininity through woman. For the "pure" male and the "pure" female have nothing in common and no means of communication with each other. They are cultural stereotypes and affectations. What a *real* man or woman is always remains inconceivable, since their reality lies in nature, not in the verbal world of concepts.

Sexual equality therefore implies a sexual life which is free from, but not against, the profane definitions of man and woman. It implies that they do not need to play roles in loving each other, but enter into a relationship for which we may borrow words which St. Augustine used in another context, "Love—and do what you will." Given the open and mutually considerate attitude of attention to each other, they are in a situation where, without restraint, "anything goes."

Role-playing is so automatic that we seldom notice how deeply it pervades our lives, and readily confuse its attitudes with our own natural and genuine inclinations. This is so much so that the love relationship is often far more of an "act" than anything else. Love itself is frequently an assumed emotion which we believe we ought to feel. Its presence is supposed to be identifiable by certain known symptoms which men and women learn to expect in each other, and which we are very clever at imitating in such a way that the right hand does not know what the left is doing. Lovers are expected to be jealous of one another. The man is supposed to act protectively and the woman a little helplessly. The man is supposed to take the initiative in expressing love and the woman to wait longingly for his attentions. Certain types of feature, voice, and figure are supposed to be peculiarly lovable or sex-appealing, and the intimacies of sexual intercourse are governed by rituals in which the man is active and the woman passive, and in which the verbal and symbolic communications of love adhere to an extremely limited pattern.

Nor is this all, for roles lie within roles like the layers of an onion. The man playing husband to wife may also be playing son to mother, or the woman daughter to father. Or the normal role-playing may be dropped deliberately so as to assume the role of "naturalness," "sincerity," or "emancipatedness." Lustfulness itself may be subconsciously cultivated so that the man may assure himself that he is really male and gets from women the socially expected thrills and excitements. More than often we make love to prove that we are lovable, which is to say that we *can* identify ourselves with a role which is conventionally acceptable.

Anyone who becomes conscious of role-playing will swiftly discover that just about *all* his attitudes are roles, that he cannot find out what he is genuinely, and is therefore at a loss what to do to express himself sincerely. Thereupon he is self-conscious and blocked in his relationships, finding himself in the double-bind predicament where every road is closed. This leaves him in a state of complete paralysis if he persists in thinking that there is some "right" course of action and some particular set of feelings which constitute his real self. Where he expected to find the specific truth about himself he found freedom, but mistook it for mere nothingness. For human freedom does indeed comprise an order, yet because it is the nonlinear order of *li* and of the Tao, it cannot be classified; it cannot be identified with any particular role. Therefore at this point of the double bind he must wait, and see what happens of itself, spontaneously. He will find that the sensation that every road is barred abruptly switches into the sensation that every road is open. He can play all roles, just as in Hindu mythology the true self is pictured as the godhead acting all the parts of the multitude of finite creatures.

Strictly speaking, it is not quite true that one must *wait* for something to happen spontaneously. For the heart is beating, the breath is moving, and all the senses are perceiving. A whole world of experience is coming to the organism of itself, without the slightest forcing. This spontaneous arrival of experience is not actually passive; it is already spontaneous *action*. When it is watched and felt to be action in this sense, it flows naturally into further action. But blocking takes place if this action is ignored and its apparent passivity interpreted as "nothing happening." It is true that it may not be what was expected to happen, but then the expected is always liable to be forced rather than spontaneous. The constant action of spontaneous experiencing which, considered as an act, is the organism's creation of its world and the world's creation of the organism, is the basis and style of action from which love and its expressions arise. In this open and ungrasping mode of awareness the beloved, the other, is not possessed but is rather received into oneself with all the richness and splendor of the unpremeditated surprise.

In almost every culture love is an intimacy between two particular people in which conventions that govern other relationships are set aside. In this respect it already suggests, even if only symbolically, the sacred rather than the profane, and the lovers' removal of clothes in one another's presence is already a sign of taking off the personal mask and stepping out of role. Only a society which is seriously ignorant of the sacred could regard the taboo, the secrecy of love, as a cloak hiding an unfortunate but necessary reversion to animality. But this is just what would be expected in a culture which conceives of spirit as other than nature, and which tries to dominate the order of nature with the order of the word. To such a mentality the identification of sexuality with the sacred is a far more serious threat than the most crass and brutish bawdiness. Its censorship can tolerate sexuality so long as it is a matter of "dirty" jokes, or so long as it is kept at the merely physiological level of medical language, so long, in other words, as it is kept as far as possible from the sacred. The association of sexuality with the sacred conjures up the most superstitious fears and fantasies, including the suspicion that it must have something to do with Satanism and the weird practices of black magic and the left-hand path!

But if the union of lovers is already a symbolic transition from the profane to the sacred, from role to reality, it is a relationship peculiarly fitted for the actual realization of liberation from *maya*. Yet this can happen only if the minds and senses of the participants are in the state of open attention whereby nature is received in its unknown reality, since closed or strained attention can perceive only its projection of the known. Here is the ideal sphere for the type of awareness which Freud considered essential for psychoanalysis.

> For as soon as attention is deliberately concentrated in a certain degree, one begins to select from the material before one; one point will be fixed in the mind with particular clearness and some other consequently disregarded, and in this selection one's expectations or one's inclinations will be followed. This is just what must not be done, however; if one's expectations are followed in this selection there is danger of never finding anything but what is already known, and if one follows one's inclinations anything which is to be perceived will most certainly be falsified.[13]

It is commonly thought that, of all people, lovers behold one another in the most unrealistic light, and that in their encounter is but the mutual projection of extravagant ideals. But may it not be that nature has allowed them to see for the first time what a human being is, and that the subsequent disillusion is not the fading of dream into reality but the strangling of reality with an all too eager embrace?

[13] Freud (2), p. 324.

8: Consummation

LOVE BRINGS THE REAL, AND NOT JUST THE
ideal, vision of what others are because it is a glimpse of
what we are bodily. For what is ordinarily called the body
is an abstraction. It is the conventional fiction of an object seen apart from its relation to the universe, without
which it has no reality whatsoever. But the mysterious and
unsought uprising of love is the experience of complete
relationship with another, transforming our vision not only
of the beloved but of the whole world. And so it remains
until the relationship is itself abstracted by the anxiety of
the grasping mind to be guarded from the rest of life as a
possession.

The bodily and the physical is not to be mistaken for
the world of atomic and discrete entities, and bodily union
must not be confined to things so obviously visible as the
juncture of Siamese twins. We need to recognize the physical reality of relationship between organisms as having as
much "substance" as the organisms themselves, if not
more. Thus however defective its doctrine of marriage in
many respects, the Christian Church is perfectly correct
in saying that husband and wife are one flesh. It is similarly correct to think of the members of the Church as the
Body of Christ, especially if the Church is considered to
be the process of realizing that the whole universe is the
Body of Christ—which is what the doctrine of the Incarnation really implies.[1]

[1] Thus St. Cyril of Alexandria in *Epist. ad Rom.*, vi, says that in a sense
the flesh of Christ "contained all nature, just as when Adam incurred

This makes it the more strange that conventional spirituality rejects the bodily union of man and woman as the most fleshly, animal, and degrading phase of human activity—a rejection showing the extent of its faulty perception and its misinterpretation of the natural world. It rejects the most concrete and creative form of man's relation to the world outside his organism, because it is through the love of a woman that he can say not only of her but also of all that is other, "This is my body."

Despite the Christian intuition of the world as the Body of Christ, the natural universe has been considered apart from and even opposed to God because it has not been experienced as one body. Considered as nothing more than a multiplicity of transient bodies, it appears that the natural world is finite and contingent upon something other than itself. No part of it remains, no part of it *is* being but only *has* being, and if the whole is only the sum of the parts, the whole cannot exist of itself. But all this comes from the failure to see that individual bodies are only the terms, the end-points, of relationships—in short, that the world is a system of inseparable relationships and not a mere juxtaposition of things. The verbal, piecemeal, and analytic mode of perception has blinded us to the fact that things and events do not exist apart from each other. The world is a whole greater than the sum of its parts because the parts are not merely summed—thrown together —but related. The whole is a pattern which remains, while the parts come and go, just as the human body is a dynamic pattern which persists despite the rapid birth and death of all its individual cells. The pattern does not, of course, exist disembodiedly apart from individual forms, but exists precisely through their coming and going—just as it is

condemnation the whole of nature contracted the disease of his curse in him."

through the structured motion and vibration of its elec-
trons that a rock has solidity.

The naïve philosophical thinking upon which Western
theology was founded assumed that what moved did not
fully exist, since true existence must be stable and static.
We see now that being and motion, mass and energy, are
inseparable, and need no longer assume that what moves
and changes is a defective form of reality. We can see that
the eternal *is* the transient, for the changing panorama of
sense experience is not just a sum of appearing and disap-
pearings things: it is stable pattern or relationship manifested as and by transient forms. Our difficulty is that
human consciousness has not adjusted itself to a relational
and integrated view of nature. We must see that consciousness is neither an isolated soul nor the mere function of a
single nervous system, but of that totality of interrelated
stars and galaxies which makes a nervous system possible. We must come to *feel* what we know to be true
in theory, to have a sense of ourselves compatible with
what we know about the inseparability of the parts of
nature.

In this light it will be clear that consciousness is no mere
phosphorescent scum upon the foundations of fire and
rock—a late addition to a world which is essentially unfeeling and mineral. Consciousness is rather the unfolding,
the "e-volution," of what has always been hidden in the
heart of the primordial universe of stars. For a universe
in which consciousness is no more than a statistical probability is still a universe in which consciousness is implicit.
It is in the living organism that the whole world feels: it
is only by virtue of eyes that the stars themselves are
light. Relationship is a kind of identity. The stars and human eyes are not mutually alien objects brought into relation by mere confrontation. Suns, stars, and planets pro-

vide the conditions in which and from which organisms can arise. Their peculiar structure *implies* organisms in such a way that, were there no organisms, the structure of the universe would be entirely different, and so that organisms, in their turn, imply a universe of just this structure. It is only the time lag and the immense complexity of the relations between stars and men which make it difficult to see that they imply one another just as much as man and woman, or the two poles of the earth.

The failure to realize the mutuality and bodily unity of man and the world underlies both the sensual and the ascetic attitudes. Trying to grasp the pleasure of the senses and to make their enjoyment the goal of life is already an attitude in which man feels divided from his experience, and sees it as something to be exploited and pursued. But the pleasure so gained is always fragmentary and frustrating, so that by way of reaction the ascetic gives up the pursuit, but not the sense of division which is the real root of the difficulty. He accentuates dividedness by pitting his will against the flesh, by siding with the abstract against the concrete, and so aggravates the very feeling from which the pursuit of pleasure arose. Ascetic spirituality is a symptom of the very disease which it intends to cure. Sensuality and conventional spirituality are not truly opposed; their conflict is a mock battle staged, unconsciously, by partisans to a single "conspiracy." [2]

Ascetic and sensualist alike confuse nature and "the body" with the abstract world of separate entities. Identifying themselves with the isolated individual, they feel inwardly incomplete. The sensualist tries to compensate

[2] See the marvellous discussion in L. L. Whyte (1), ch. 3, where the author attempts a physiological and historical analysis of the origins of the conflict. A current instance of this mock battle is the alliance of organized crime with conservative church groups to maintain the legal suppression of certain types of vice.

for his insufficiency by extracting pleasure, or completeness, from the world which appears to stand apart from
him as something lacking. The ascetic, with an attitude of
"sour grapes," makes a virtue of the lack. Both have failed
to distinguish between pleasure and the pursuit of pleasure, between appetite or desire and the exploitation of
desire, and to see that pleasure grasped is no pleasure.
For pleasure is a grace and is not obedient to the commands of the will. In other words, it is brought about by
the relationship between man and his world. Like mystical insight itself, it must always come unsought, which
is to say that relationship can be experienced fully only
by mind and senses which are open and not attempting
to be clutching muscles. There is obviously nothing degrading in sensuous pleasure which comes "of itself," without
craving. But in fact there is no other kind of pleasure, and
the error of the sensualist is not so much that he is doing
something evil as that he is attempting the impossible.
Naturally, it is possible to exercise the muscles in pursuing something that may, or may not, give pleasure; but
pleasure cannot be given unless the senses are in a state
of accepting rather than taking, and for this reason they
must not be, as it were, paralyzed and rigidified by the
anxiety to get something out of the object.

All this is peculiarly true of love and of the sexual communion between man and woman. This is why it has such
a strongly spiritual and mystical character when spontaneous, and why it is so degrading and frustrating when
forced. It is for this reason that sexual love is so problematic in cultures where the human being is strongly identified with the abstract separate entity. The experience
neither lives up to expectations nor fulfills the relationship
between man and woman. At the same time it is, frag-
mentarily, gratifying enough to be pursued ever more re-

lentlessly for the release which it seems to promise. Sex is therefore the virtual religion of very many people, the end to which they accord more devotion than any other. To the conventionally religious mind this worship of sex is a dangerous and positively sinful substitute for the worship of God. But this is because sex, or any other pleasure, as ordinarily pursued is never a true fulfillment. For this very reason it is *not* God, but not at all because it is "merely physical." The rift between God and nature would vanish if we knew how to experience nature, because what keeps them apart is not a difference of substance but a split in the mind.

But, as we have seen, the problems of sexuality cannot be solved at their own level. The full splendor of sexual experience does not reveal itself without a new mode of attention to the world in general. On the other hand, the sexual relationship is a setting in which the full opening of attention may rather easily be realized because it is so immediately rewarding. It is the most common and dramatic instance of union between oneself and the other. But to serve as a means of initiation to the "one body" of the universe, it requires what we have called a contemplative approach. This is not love "without desire" in the sense of love without delight, but love which is not contrived or willfully provoked as an escape from the habitual empty feeling of an isolated ego.

It is not quite correct to say that such a relationship goes far beyond the "merely sexual," for it would be better to say that sexual contact irradiates every aspect of the encounter, spreading its warmth into work and conversation outside the bounds of actual "love-making." Sexuality is not a separate compartment of human life; it is a radiance pervading every human relationship, but assuming a particular intensity at certain points. Conversely, we might say that sexuality is a special mode or degree of the total intercourse of man and nature. Its delight is an intimation of the ordinarily repressed delight which inheres in life itself, in our fundamental but normally unrealized identity with the world.

A relationship of this kind cannot adequately be discussed, as in manuals of sexual hygiene, as a matter of techniques. It is true that in Taoism and Tantric Buddhism there are what appear to be techniques or "practices" of sexual relationship, but these are, like sacraments, the "outward and visible signs of an inward and spiritual grace." Their use is the consequence rather than the cause of a certain inner attitude, since they suggest themselves almost naturally to partners who take their love as it comes, contemplatively, and are in no hurry to grasp anything from it. Sexual yoga needs to be freed from a misunderstanding attached to all forms of yoga, of spiritual "practice" or "exercise," since these ill-chosen words suggest that yoga is a method for the progressive achievement of certain results—and this is exactly what it is not.[3] Yoga means "union," that is, the realization of man's inner identity with Brahman or Tao, and strictly speaking this is not an end to which there are methods or means since it cannot be made an object of desire. The attempt to achieve it invariably thrusts it away. Yoga "practices" are therefore sacramental expressions or "celebrations" of this union, in rather the same sense that Catholics celebrate the Mass as an expression of Christ's "full, perfect, and *sufficient* sacrifice." Means are irrelevant to what is already sufficient. Thus contemplation or meditation which seeks a result is neither contemplation nor meditation, for the simple reason that contemplation (*kuan*) is consciousness without seeking. Naturally, such consciousness is concen-

[3] See the excellent discussion of this point in Guénon (1), pp. 261–67.

trated, but it is not "practicing concentration"; it is concentrated in whatever happens to be its "eternal now."

Sexual yoga or, as it is technically called, *maithuna* is a common theme of Hindu sculpture, though it has been suggested that its origins are Chinese, arriving in India as the backwash of the spread of Buddhism. Westerners, including missionaries and Theosophists and Indians under their influence, have rather naturally spread the idea that these images are pornographic, and that sexual yoga represents a perverse and depraved degeneration of Eastern spirituality. Such a reaction is only to be expected from spectators to whom the idea of spiritualized sexuality is completely unfamiliar. But such serious and responsible scholars as Woodroffe (1), S. B. Dasgupta (1), and Coomaraswamy (1) have made it plain not only that such images have no pornographic intention, but also that what they represent is at once a metaphysical doctrine and a sacrament at least as sacred as Christian matrimony. For the *maithuna* figures have nothing to do with promiscuous ritual orgies. On the one hand, they are emblems of the eternal union of spirit and nature; on the other, they represent the consummation of contemplative love between mutually dedicated partners.[4]

[4] Woodroffe (1), p. 578, states that the partners are normally husband and wife, though in special circumstances, valid in a polygynous culture, the woman is a permanent wife-in-religion chosen because of spiritual compatibility with the man. The notion that sexual yoga is involved with "black magic" is one of the many distortions of Asian philosophy circulated by Theosophy—a Westernized version of Hindu-Buddhist teachings carrying over essentially Christian notions of evil. The Theosophists were in the first place misled by the fact that practitioners of sexual yoga adhered to the "left-hand path," a nomenclature to which they attached the purely Western associations of "sinister." But in Indian symbolism the right- and left-hand paths do not depart in opposite directions: they converge upon the same point like the two halves of a circle. The right-hand path seeks liberation by detachment from the world, and the left-hand by total acceptance of the world; the right is the—symbolically—male way, and the left the female, so that

The general idea of Tantric *maithuna*, as of its Taoist counterpart, is that sexual love may be transformed into a type of worship in which the partners are, for each other, incarnations of the divine. Perhaps this statement must be somewhat modified with respect to Buddhism and Taoism, to which the notion of worship is really foreign, and one must substitute the contemplation of nature in its true state. The embrace of *maithuna* involves also a transmutation of the sexual energy which it arouses, and this is described symbolically as sending it upwards from the loins to the head. Yoga, as is well known, involves a peculiar symbolism of human anatomy in which the spinal column is seen as a figure of the Tree of Life, with its roots in the nether world and its branches, or its flower, in the heavens beneath the "firmament" of the skull. The base of the spinal-tree is the seat of *kundalini*, the Serpent Power, which is an image of the divine life-energy incarnate in nature and asleep under the illusion of *maya*. Yoga consists in awakening the Serpent and allowing it to ascend the tree to the heavens, wherefrom it passes liberated through the "sun-door" at the apex of the skull. Thus when the Serpent is at the base of the spinal-tree it manifests its power as sexual energy; when it is at the crown it manifests itself as spiritual energy.

According to Tantric symbolism, the energy of the *kundalini* is aroused but simply dissipated in ordinary

in the left man finds liberation through nature and through woman. Hence the discipline is called *sahaja*, the natural or spontaneous way. It must furthermore be remembered that Theosophical attitudes reflected the nineteenth-century prudishness of middle-class England and America. A similar confusion was the Theosophical invention of a "lodge" of *"dugpas"* or black magicians, based on what was at the time mere hearsay about the now well-known Drug-pa Sect of Tibetan Buddhism. On the complex metaphysical symbolism of *maithuna* or *yab-yum* (Tibet) figures, see S. B. Dasgupta (1), pp. 98–134. The correspondence is not always strictly that of spirit and nature, but also of wisdom (*prajna*) and activity (*upaya*), voidness (*sunyata*) and compassion (*karuna*).

sexual activity. It can, however, be transmuted in a prolonged embrace in which the male orgasm is reserved and the sexual energy diverted into contemplation of the divine as incarnate in the woman.[5] The partners are therefore seated in the cross-legged posture of meditation, the woman clasping the man's waist with her thighs and her arms about his neck. Such a position is clearly unsuitable for motion, the point being that the partners should remain still and so prolong the embrace that the exchange between them would be passive and receptive rather than active. Nothing is *done* to excite the sexual energy; it is simply allowed to follow its own course without being "grasped" or exploited by the imagination and the will. In the meantime the mind and senses are not given up to fantasy, but remain simply open to "what is," without —as we should say in current slang—trying to make something of it.

In trying to understand anything of this kind, the modern Westerner must be careful not to confuse the symbology of the *kundalini* and the ascension of the sexual force with any physiological situation. Indeed, anatomical symbolisms of this kind are so strange to us that they hinder rather than help our comprehension of the real intent. Furthermore, almost all ancient sexual ideas are bound up with notions of the semen and its properties which we no longer share, and thus we do not regard it as a vital fluid to be conserved like blood. Our physiology does not support the idea that the male orgasm is a debilitating leakage of strength, and therefore the mere avoidance of the orgasm will have little significance in any modern application of sexual yoga.

---

[5] The Taoist practice permits the orgasm in due course, and the female orgasm was felt to nourish and strengthen the male force. See Needham (1), vol. 2, pp. 149–50.

The importance of these ancient ideas to us lies not so much in their technicalities as in their psychological intent. They express an attitude to sexuality which, if absorbed by us today, could contribute more than anything else to the healing of the confusion and frustration of our marital and sexual relations. It remains, then, to separate the underlying sexual philosophy of Tantra and Taoism from symbolic and ritual elements which have no meaning for us, and to see whether it can be applied in terms of our own culture.

To clarify the basic intent of sexual yoga we must study its practice in context with the underlying principles of Buddhist and Taoist philosophy. For Buddhism the basic principle is to have one's consciousness undisturbed by *trishna,* or grasping desire, in such a way that the senses do not receive a distorted and fragmentary vision of the world. For Taoism the principle differs only in terminology: it is *wu-wei,* or noninterference with the Tao or course of nature, which is the organic and spontaneous functioning of man-in-relation-to-his-environment. Both involve the contemplative or open-sensed attitude to experience, the Buddhist *dhyana* (in Japanese, *zen*) and the Taoist *kuan.* In their respective yogas, both practice "watching over the breath" because the rhythm of breathing determines the total disposition of the organism. Now, their attitude to breathing is one of the main keys to understanding their attitude to sexuality.

According to some accounts, perfect mastery of the breath is attained when its rhythm comes to a total stop —without loss of life. This is obviously a literalistic caricature, based on a crude version of the meaning of *nirvana* —"breathed out." Actually, "watching over the breath" consists in letting the breath come and go as it wants, without forcing it or clutching at it. In due course its rhythm automatically slows down, and it flows in and out so smoothly that all rasping and hissing ceases *as if* it had stopped. This is both a symbol of and a positive aid to letting one's whole life come and go without grasping, since the way a person breathes is indicative of the way he lives.

In the sexual sphere the stopping of the male orgasm is just as much of a literalism as the stopping of breath; the point in both instances is not to stop but not to grasp. As contemplation of the breathing process automatically slows it down, sexual contemplation naturally delays the orgasm. For there is no value in prolonged and motionless intercourse as such; the point is to allow the sexual process to become spontaneous, and this cannot happen without the prior disappearance of the ego—of the forcing of sexual pleasure. Thus the orgasm is spontaneous (*tzu-jan*) when it happens of itself and in its own time, and when the rest of the body moves *in response* to it. Active or forced sexual intercourse is the deliberate imitation of movements which should ordinarily come about of themselves. Given the open attitude of mind and senses, sexual love in this spirit is a revelation. Long before the male orgasm begins, the sexual impulse manifests itself as what can only be described, psychologically, as a melting warmth between the partners so that they seem veritably to flow into each other. To put it in another way, "physical lust" transforms itself into the most considerate and tender form of love imaginable.

A valuable attempt to work out something of this kind for modern conditions has been made by von Urban (1), but for these purposes his approach is too much at the level of sexual hygiene and too preoccupied with technical directions that are somewhat inelastic and compulsive. Furthermore, just as the Tantric discussions are overlaid with their elaborate anatomical symbolism, von Urban has introduced some highly speculative ideas about electrical exchanges between sexual partners which resemble the "orgone" theories of Reich (1). But mechanistic symbolisms of mysterious "forces" and "fluids," to account for the intense feeling of interchange between the partners, are unnecessary in a philosophy of nature which gives due weight to the fact that organisms exist only by relation to each other and to their environment. Sexual love in the contemplative spirit simply provides the conditions in which we can be aware of our mutual interdependence and "oneness."

The point is so important that it can bear repetition: contemplative love—like contemplative meditation—is only quite secondarily a matter of technique. For it has no specific aim; there is nothing particular that has to be made to happen. It is simply that a man and a woman are together exploring their spontaneous feeling—without any preconceived idea of what it ought to be, since the sphere of contemplation is not what should be but what *is*. In a world of clocks and schedules the one really important technical item is the provision of adequate time. Yet this is not so much clock time as psychological time, the attitude of letting things happen in their own time, and of an ungrasping and unhurrying interchange of the senses with their objects. In default of this attitude the greater part of sexual experience in our culture falls far short of its possibilities.[6] The encounter is brief, the fe-

---

[6] Kinsey (1), p. 580, states that "for perhaps three-quarters of all males, orgasm is reached within two minutes after the initiation of the sexual relation, and for a not inconsiderable number of males the climax may be reached within less than a minute or even within ten or twenty seconds after coital entrance." He goes on to point out that this seems natural enough if man be compared with other mammals, but that unfortunately this makes it difficult for most women to experience the orgasm. He feels, therefore, that it is "demanding that the male be quite abnormal in his ability to prolong sexual activity without ejaculation if

male orgasm relatively rare, and the male orgasm precipitate or "forced" by premature motion. By contrast, the
contemplative and inactive mode of intercourse makes it
possible to prolong the interchange almost indefinitely,
and to delay the male orgasm without discomfort or the
necessity of diverting full attention from the situation.
Furthermore, when the man has become accustomed to
this approach, it is possible also for him to engage in active
intercourse for a very much longer period, so affording
the greatest possible stimulation for the woman.[7]

One of the first phases of contemplative love is the discovery of the depth and satisfaction of very simple contacts
which are ordinarily called "preliminaries" to sexual activity. But in a relationship which has no goal other than
itself, nothing is merely preliminary. One finds out what it
can mean simply to look at the other person, to touch
hands, or to listen to the voice. If these contacts are not
regarded as leading to something else, but rather allowed
to come to one's consciousness as if the source of activity
lay in them and not in the will, they become sensations of
immense subtlety and richness. Received thus, the ex-

he is required to match the female partner." It has been pointed out by
Ford and Beach (1), pp. 30–31, that we have little evidence to show the
extent of the female orgasm among mammals, but that it is supposedly
rare or absent among the primates. However, the considerable physical
differences between man and the higher mammals require caution in
using these species to determine what is "natural" for man. Kinsey's
statistical estimates, so often questioned, may be compared with those
of Dickinson and Beam (1), quoted by Ford and Beach, p. 32, giving
the duration of intercourse of a sample of 362 American couples as less
than 10 minutes for 74 per cent and less than 20 minutes for 91 per cent.
[7] *Karezza*, or intercourse without the male orgasm (*coitus reservatus*),
is also possible in this way, though there is considerable difference of
opinion as to its psychological healthiness, especially when used frequently as a means of contraception. Possible psychological dangers are
perhaps diminished by the great satisfaction of sexual contact alone in
the contemplative mood. However the "spirituality" of *karezza* is con-
nected with unverified notions about the sublimation of the semen and
the loss of psychic "power" involved in its ejaculation.

ternal world acquires a liveliness which one ordinarily associates only with one's own bodily activity, and from this
comes the sensation that one's body somehow includes the
external world.

It was through the practice of *za-zen* or "sitting meditation" in this particular attitude that Japanese Zen Buddhists
discovered the possibilities of such arts as the tea cere-
mony (*cha-no-yu*), wherein the most intense aesthetic
delight is found in the simplest social association of drink-
ing tea with a few friends. For the art developed into a
contemplation of the unexpected beauty in the "primitive" and unpretentious utensils employed, and in the
natural simplicity of the surroundings—the unchiselled
mountain rocks in the garden, the texture of paper walls,
and the grain of rough wooden beams. Obviously, the cultivation of this viewpoint can lead to an infinitely refined
snobbery when it is done with an eye to oneself doing
it—when, in other words, the point becomes not the objects of contemplation but the "exercise" of contemplating.
For this reason, lovers who begin to relate themselves to
each other in this way need not feel that they are practicing a skill in which there are certain standards of excel-
lence which they *ought* to attain. It is simply absurd for
them to sit down and *restrain* themselves just to looking at
each other, while fighting off the intense desire to fall into
each other's arms. The point is to discover the wonder of
simple contacts, not the duty of it, for which reason it may
be better at first to explore this type of relationship after
intercourse than before.

The fact remains, however, that if they let themselves
come gradually and gently into contact, they create a situation in which their senses can really work, so that when
they have discovered what it can mean just to touch hands,
the intimacy of a kiss or even of lips in near proximity re-

gains the "electric" quality which it had at the first meeting. In other words, they find out what the kiss *really* involves, just as profound love reveals what other people really are: beings in relation, not in isolation.

If we say that from such contacts the movement toward sexual intercourse grows of itself, it may be supposed that this is no more than what ordinarily happens. Intimacy just leads to passion; it certainly does not have to be willed. But there is all the difference in the world between gobbling and actually tasting food when one is hungry. It is not merely that appetite needs restraint; it needs awareness—awareness of the total process of the organism-environment moving into action of itself. As the lead and response of good dancers appears to be almost simultaneous, as if they were a single entity, there comes a moment when more intimate sexual contact occurs with an extraordinary mutuality. The man does not lead and the woman follow; the man-and-woman relationship acts of itself. The feeling of this mutuality is entirely distinct from that of a man initiating sexual contact with a perfectly willing woman. His "advance" and her "response" seems to be the *same* movement.

At a particular but unpredetermined moment they may, for example, take off their clothes as if the hands of each belonged to the other. The gesture is neither awkward nor bold; it is the simultaneous expression of a unity beneath the masks of social roles and proprieties by the revelation and contact of the intimate and off-scene aspects of their bodies. Now, these aspects are ordinarily guarded because of their extreme sensitivity, or awareness of relationship. Only the eyes are as sensitive, and in ordinary social intercourse prolonged eye-contact is avoided because of its embarrassing intimacy—embarrassing because it creates a sense of relationship belying and overpassing the separative roles which we take so much trouble to maintain. For the sensitive organs of the body which we call most intimate and private are not, as might be supposed, the most central to the ego. On the contrary, they are those which most surpass the ego because their sensitivity brings the greatest contact with the outside world, the greatest intimacy with what is formally "other."

The psychic counterpart of this bodily and sensuous intimacy is a similar openness of attention to each other's thoughts—a form of communion which can be as sexually "charged" as physical contact. This is the feeling that one can express one's thoughts to the other just as they are, since there is not the slightest compulsion to assume a pretended character. This is perhaps the rarest and most difficult aspect of any human relationship, since in ordinary social converse the spontaneous arising of thought is more carefully hidden than anything else. Between unconscious and humorless people who do not know and accept their own limitations it is almost impossible, for the things which we criticize most readily in others are usually those of which we are least conscious in ourselves. Yet this is quite the most important part of a deep sexual relationship, and it is in some way understood even when thoughts are left unsaid.[8]

[8] Obviously, we are speaking here of a very special relationship which is seldom to be found in the ordinary marriage contracted between emotionally immature and socially rigid people, when the more mature partner should express his or her mind only with the utmost consideration for the other. Complete self-expression is really a form of self-indulgence in circumstances where it cannot be received. While it may sometimes be "good" for another person to be frank with them, husbands and wives should be the last people to take on programs of mutual improvement. It may be cynical, but it is good-naturedly and humanly so, to assume that one's spouse is going to remain just as he or she is, and that one is going to have to live with these limitations. If they are going to change at all, this is the only way to begin. For this is already an act of deep acceptance of the other person, which may become mutual by a kind of psychic osmosis.

It is significant that we commonly say that those with whom we can express ourselves most spontaneously are those with whom we can most fully be ourselves. For this already implies that the full and real self is not the willing and deliberating function but the spontaneous. In the same way that our most sensitive organs are guarded because they transcend and break the bonds of the ego, the flow of thought and feeling—though called one's "inner self"— is the most spontaneous and role-free activity of all. The more inward and central the form of activity, the less it partakes of the mask of the ego. To unveil the flow of thought can therefore be an even greater sexual intimacy than physical nakedness.

In contemplative love we do not speak of the sexual "act," since this puts intercourse into its own special dis- sociated compartment, where it becomes what Albert Jay Nock called very properly and humorously the "cul- batising exercise." Perhaps one of the subordinate reasons why sex is a matter for laughter is that there is something ridiculous in "doing" it with set purpose and deliberation —even when described with so picturesque a phrase as the Chinese "flowery combat." Without wanting to make rules for this freest of all human associations, it is certainly best to approach it inactively. For when the couple are so close to each other that the sexual parts are touching, it is only necessary to remain quietly and unhurriedly still, so that in time the woman can absorb the man's member into herself without being actively penetrated.[9]

[9] Von Urban (1) does not recommend the cross-legged "Tantric" posture, which is naturally difficult for those not used to sitting in this way. In- stead, he suggests lying at right angles to each other, the woman on her back with one leg between the man's thighs and the other resting on his hip. In this way the contact is purely genital and the whole relation- ship between the two "pours through" this center. While this is an excellent way of beginning, there is no need to make it a fixed rule, though there is an extraordinary intensity in letting the whole feeling-

It is at this juncture that simple waiting with open attention is most rewarding. If no attempt is made to induce the orgasm by bodily motion, the interpenetration of the sexual centers becomes a channel of the most vivid psychic interchange. While neither partner is working to make anything happen, both surrender themselves completely to whatever the process itself may feel like doing. The sense of identity with the other becomes peculiarly intense, though it is rather as if a new identity were formed between them with a life of its own. This life—one might say this Tao—lifts them out of themselves so that they feel carried together upon a stream of vitality which can only be called cosmic, because it is no longer what "you" and "I" are doing. Although the man does nothing either to excite or withhold the orgasm, it becomes possible to let this interchange continue for an hour or more, during which the female orgasm may occur several times with a very slight amount of active stimulation, depending upon the degree of her receptivity to the experience as a process taking charge of her.

In due course, both partners feel relieved of all anxiety as to whether orgasm will or will not happen, which makes it possible for them to give themselves up to whatever forms of sexual play may suggest themselves, however active or even violent. We say "suggest themselves" because this is a matter of immediate feeling rather than learned technique—a response to the marvellously overwhelming urge to turn themselves inside out for each other. Or it may happen that they prefer simply to remain still and let the process unfold itself at the level of pure feeling, which usually tends to be the deeper and more psychically satisfying way.

relationship pass through the sexual centers alone. The "absorption" of the male member depends, of course, upon the sufficient secretion of vaginal moisture.

Feelings which at the height of intercourse are often taken for the extremity of lust—that question-begging word—are simply the *ananda,* the ecstasy of bliss, which accompanies the experience of relationship as distinct from isolated selfhood. "Abandon" expresses the mood better than "lust," because the two individuals give themselves up to the process or relationship between them, and this abandonment of wills can become so intense that it feels like the desire to give up life itself—to die into the other person. De Rougemont (1) maintains—I think wrongly—that this "death wish" distinguishes mere passion or *eros* from divine love or *agape.* He feels that the former, being a purely creaturely love, seeks the nonbeing which was its origin, and that the latter is the love of the Creator which seeks life because its origin is pure Being. This entirely neglects the Christian mystery of Death and Resurrection, which is the Christian version of the more widely held truth that death and life are not opposed, but mutually arising aspects of a Whole—so that life emerges from plunging into death, and death from plunging into life. But the death wish in love is figurative, the giving up of life being a poetic image for the mystical, self-transcending quality of sexual transport. Death in the same figurative sense, as "dying to oneself," is commonly used in mystical literature for the process whereby the individual becomes divine. It is no more literal than the "death" of a grain of corn planted in the soil, or of a caterpillar sleeping in its chrysalis.

The mood of intense sexual delight is not, however, always quite so overwhelming as a desire to "die." The sense of "abandon" or of being carried out of oneself may equally find expression in gaiety, and this is peculiarly true when the experience brings a strong sense of fulfillment. Rare as such gaiety may be in cultures where there is a tie between sex and guilt, the release from self brings laughter in love-making as much as in mysticism, for we must remember that it was Dante who described the song of the angels in heaven as "the laughter of the universe." "Love," said Coventry Patmore, "raises the spirit above the sphere of reverence and worship into one of laughter and dalliance." This is above all true when the partners are not *working* at their love to be sure that they attain a "real experience." The grasping approach to sexuality destroys its gaiety before anything else, blocking up its deepest and most secret fountain. For there is really no other reason for creation than pure joy.

It is no matter for timing by the clock how long this play should continue. Let it be repeated again, its timeless quality is not attained by endurance or even duration, but by absence of purpose and hurry. The final release of orgasm, neither sought nor restrained, is simply allowed to "come," as even the popular expression suggests from our intuitive knowledge that it is not a deed but a gift and a grace. When this experience bursts in upon fully opened feelings it is no mere "sneeze in the loins" relieving physical tension: it is an explosion whose outermost sparks are the stars.

This may seem irreverent, or just claiming too much, to those who are unwilling to feel it completely, refusing to see anything mystical or divine in the moment of life's origin. Yet it is just in treating this moment as a bestial convulsion that we reveal our vast separation from life. It is just at this extreme point that we must find the physical and the spiritual to be one, for otherwise our mysticism is sentimental or sterile-pure and our sexuality just vulgar. Without—in its true sense—the lustiness of sex, religion is joyless and abstract; without the self-abandonment of religion, sex is a mechanical masturbation.

The height of sexual love, coming upon us of itself, is one

of the most total experiences of relationship to the other
of which we are capable, but prejudice and insensitivity
have prevented us from seeing that in any other circumstances such delight would be called mystical ecstasy. For
what lovers feel for each other in this moment is no other
than adoration in its full religious sense, and its climax is
almost literally the pouring of their lives into each other.
Such adoration, which is due only to God, would indeed
be idolatrous were it not that in that moment love takes
away illusion and shows the beloved for what he or she
in truth is—not the socially pretended person but the naturally divine.

Mystical vision, as has always been recognized, does not
remain at the peak of ecstasy. As in love, its ecstasy leads
into clarity and peace. The aftermath of love is an anti-
climax only when the climax has been taken and not received. But when the whole experience was received the
aftermath finds one in a marvellously changed and yet
unchanged world, and here we are speaking of spirituality and sexuality in the same breath. For the mind and
senses do not now have to open themselves; they find
themselves naturally opened, and it appears that the divine world is no other than the everyday world. Just as
they come and just as they are, the simplest sights and
sounds are sufficient, and do not have to be brushed aside
in the mind's eagerness to find something more significant.
One is thereby initiated from the world of clock time to
the world of real time, in which events come and go of
themselves in unforced succession—timed by themselves
and not by the mind. As the accomplished singer does not
sing a song but lets it sing itself with his voice—since
otherwise he will lose the rhythm and strain the tone—
the course of life is here seen to happen of itself, in a continuum where the active and the passive, the inward and

the outward are the same. Here we have at last found the true place of man in nature which underlies the imagery of the Chinese poem:

> *Let us live*
> *Among the white clouds and scarlet woodlands,*
> *Singing together*
> *Songs of the Great Peace.*[10]

[10] *Teiwa shu, ii.* Tr. Ruth Sasaki, in *Zen Notes*, III, 10. New York, 1956.

Bibliographical References

This is neither a bibliography of the subject of this book nor a list of works read in its preparation, but simply a reference list of sources mentioned or quoted.

BATESON, G., with JACKSON, D. D., HALEY, J., and WEAK-LAND, J. H. "Towards a Theory of Schizophrenia," *Behavioral Science*, vol. I, 4. October, 1956. Pp. 251–64.

BONPENSIERE, L. *New Pathways in Piano Technique*. Philosophical Library, New York, 1953.

BURROW, T. *Science and Man's Behavior*. Philosophical Library, New York, 1953.

CH'U TA-KAO. *Tao Te Ching*. The Buddhist Society, London, 1937.

COOMARASWAMY, A. K. *The Dance of Shiva*. Noonday Press, New York, 1957.

DASGUPTA, S. B. *An Introduction to Tantric Buddhism*. University of Calcutta Press, 1950.

DE ROUGEMONT, D. *Love in the Western World*. Pantheon Books, New York, 1956.

DICKINSON, R. L., and BEAM, L. *A Thousand Marriages*. Williams and Wilkins, Baltimore, 1931.

DODS, M. *The City of God* (St. Augustine). 2 vols. Clark, Edinburgh, 1872.

ECKERMANN, J. P. *Conversations of Goethe*. J. M. Dent, London, 1930.

ELLIS, H. *Studies in the Psychology of Sex*. 2-vol. ed. Random House, New York, 1942.

EVANS, C. de B. *Meister Eckhart*. 2 vols. Watkins, London, 1924.

FORD, C. S., and BEACH, F. A. *Patterns of Sexual Behavior*. Harper, New York, 1951.

FREUD, S. (1) *Civilization and Its Discontents*. Hogarth Press, London, 1949.

(2) *Collected Papers*. Vol. 2. Hogarth Press, London, 1924.

FUNG YU-LAN. *History of Chinese Philosophy.* 2 vols. Princeton University Press, 1953.

GILES, H. A. *Chuang-tzu.* Kelly and Walsh, Shanghai, 1926.

GILES, L. *Taoist Teachings.* Translations from Lieh-tzu. John Murray, London, 1925.

GUÉNON, R. *Introduction to the Study of the Hindu Doctrines.* Luzac, London, 1945.

HUME, D. *Treatise of Human Nature.* Oxford University Press, 1946.

JUNG, C. G. *Answer to Job.* Routledge, London, 1954.

KINSEY, A. C., POMEROY, W. B., and MARTIN, C. E. *Sexual Behavior in the Human Male.* Saunders, Philadelphia and London, 1948.

LIN YUTANG. (1) *My Country and My People.* Halcyon House, New York, 1938.

(2) *The Wisdom of Lao-tse.* Modern Library, New York, 1948.

NEEDHAM, J. *Science and Civilization in China.* Vol. 2. Cambridge University Press, 1956.

NORTHROP, F. S. C. *The Meeting of East and West.* Macmillan, New York, 1946.

REICH, W. *The Function of the Orgasm.* Orgone Institute Press, New York, 1948.

SIU, R. G. H. *The Tao of Science.* John Wiley, New York, 1957.

SUZUKI, D. T. (1) *Essays in Zen Buddhism.* Vol. 2. London and Kyoto, 1933. Repr., Rider, London, 1950.

(2) *Manual of Zen Buddhism.* Kyoto, 1935. Repr., Rider, London, 1950.

(3) *Training of the Zen Buddhist Monk.* Eastern Buddhist Society, Kyoto, 1934.

TAYLOR, G. R. *Sex in History.* Thames and Hudson, London, 1954.

VATSYAYANA. *Le Kama Soutra (Kamasutra).* J. Fort, Paris, n. d.

VON URBAN, R. *Sex Perfection and Marital Happiness.* Dial Press, New York, 1955.

WALEY, A. *The Nō Plays of Japan.* Allen and Unwin, London, 1950.

WATTS, A. W. (1) *The Supreme Identity.* Noonday Press, New York, 1957.

(2) *Myth and Ritual in Christianity.* Thames and Hudson, London, and Vanguard, New York, 1954.

WELCH, H. *The Parting of the Way.* Beacon Press, Boston, 1957.

WHITEHEAD, A. N. *Science and the Modern World.* Cambridge University Press, 1933.

WHYTE, L. L. *The Next Development in Man.* Henry Holt, New York, 1948.

WOODROFFE, Sir J. *Shakti and Shakta.* Luzac, London, 1929.

ZIMMER, H. (1) *Myths and Symbols in Indian Art and Civilization.* Pantheon Books (Bollingen Series), New York, 1946.

(2) *Philosophies of India.* Pantheon Books (Bollingen Series), New York, 1951.

(3) *The Art of Indian Asia.* 2 vols. Pantheon Books (Bollingen Series), New York, 1955.

ALAN W. WATTS, who held both a master's degree in theology and a doctorate of divinity, is best known as an interpreter of Zen Buddhism in particular, and of Indian and Chinese philosophy in general. Standing apart, however, from sectarian membership, he has earned the reputation of being one of the most original and "unrutted" philosophers of the century. He was the author of some twenty books on the philosophy and psychology of religion, including (in Vintage Books) *The Way of Zen; The Joyous Cosmology; The Wisdom of Insecurity; Behold the Spirit; The Book; Does It Matter?; This Is It; The Supreme Identity; Beyond Theology;* and *Cloud Hidden, Whereabouts Unknown.* He died in 1973.